Forlorn Hope:
Regimental Wargame Scenarios for the Mississippi River Campaigns: 1861-1863

By Brad Butkovich

Forlorn Hope: Regimental Wargame Scenarios for the Mississippi River Campaigns: 1861-1863
Copyright © 2024 Historic Imagination LLC
All rights reserved.

"All our field-batteries were put in position, and were covered by good epaulements; the troops were brought forward, in easy support, concealed by the shape of the ground; and to the minute, viz., 10 a. m. of May 22d, the troops sprang to the assault. A small party, that might be called a forlorn hope, provided with plank to cross the ditch, advanced at a run, up to the very ditch; the lines of infantry sprang from cover, and advanced rapidly in line of battle.
Major General William T. Sherman, commander Fifteenth Army Corps, of actions outside of Vicksburg, Mississippi, May 22nd.

"The 'Forlorn Hope' had commenced the charge, O'Brien saying, 'Come boys! pick up your bundles and follow me,' and General Augur gave the command, 'Forward the Brigade,' and the whole brigade advanced into the 'slashings.'"
Albert Plummer, 48th Massachusetts Regimental History, of actions at Port Hudson, Louisiana May 27th, 1863.

Stock #: HI020
ISBN 979-8-9904149-1-4

Cover: The Stockade Redan at Vicksburg from the Union approaches along the Graveyard Road.

All images of personalities were taken from the National Archives and Records Administration or the Library of Congress and are public domain due to age and expiration of copyright. All modern images of the battlefield were taken by the author.

All modern battlefield images are © 2024 Historic Imagination.

This book may not be reproduced in any format.

Historic Imagination LLC
4025 Leeambur Court
Lilburn, GA 30047
www.historicimagination.com

Table of Contents

Introduction 5

How to Use This Book 7

The Battle of Belmont 13

The Battle of Baton Rouge 21

The Battle of Chickasaw Bayou 29

The Battle of Champion Hill: The Crossroads 39

The Battle of Champion Hill: The Coker House 51

The Battle of Big Black River Bridge 59

Vicksburg Assault: Sherman May 19th 67

Vicksburg Assault: Sherman May 22nd 75

Vicksburg Assault: McPherson May 22nd 85

Vicksburg Assault: McClernand May 22nd 95

Port Hudson Assault: Northern Flank 105

Port Hudson Assault: Eastern Flank 115

The Battle of Milliken's Bend 121

The Battle of Lake Providence 129

The Battle of Helena 135

Introduction

The Mississippi River was the superhighway of North America until the industrialization of the late 19th Century. A merchant or supplier from St. Paul, Minnesota, Pittsburg, Pennsylvania, or even Chief Looking's Village at present day Bismarck, North Dakota could send their goods downstream to the port of New Orleans, to find overseas buyers. The river and its massive watershed was the economic lifeblood of the American interior.

It's little wonder that the formation of the Confederate States of America and its new control over the Mighty Mississippi sent shockwaves through the North. If allowed to remain, Confederate control of the river, with its inevitable fees and tariffs for river traffic, would put a significant burden on commerce in the North. As such, the opening of the river to unimpeded traffic was a major early goal of the Union military and civilian leadership.

The battles along and for control of the river began immediately. General Ulysses S. Grant started his career in a raid near Belmont, Missouri in late 1861. Admiral David G. Farragut captured New Orleans at the mouth of the river in April and May, 1862, then dashed up the river to Vicksburg. Twice in May and June he attempted to force the surrender of the key city, which stood on high bluffs and controlled all traffic on the river, but failed. Thus began a series of land campaigns that culminated in Grant marching around the city's defenses and attacking from the landward side. In July 1863, both Vicksburg and Port Hudson to the south finally fell to the Union, and as President Abraham Lincoln declared, "The Father of Waters again goes unvexed to the sea."

This scenario book contains rules to play fifteen battles for control of the Mississippi River during the American Civil War. The games offer a variety of tactical situations from maneuver, to urban warfare (a rarity!), and of course, assaulting the works along the Vicksburg line. Game sizes range from small to large. From a small brigade per side to commanding a corps in the heat of battle. Can you free the Mississippi River for the Union, or hold back the blue tide as the Confederates?

No specific set of rules is required to play the games in this book. Each scenario includes a detailed map for placing terrain and scenery on the game table. Unit starting locations are clearly marked, as well as where reinforcements may enter the board. Time is expressed in terms of 10 minute, 15 minute, and 20 minute increments; easily adaptable to most regimental level rules. The scenarios also provide a detailed Order of Battle showing each unit that fought in that battle, including figure ratios for 20, 30, 40, 50, and 100 historic men per figure/stand. The Order of Battle also includes a rating for each unit, as well as the weapons they carried into battle.

I wish to thank Scott Felsen for his help traveling to many of these small battlefields to do research and take pictures. I also would like to thank Kimberly Schwatka for her research in the National Archives that gathered most of the records on which to base the Union regimental strengths.

I hope you enjoy the book. Have fun at the game table!

How to Use This Book

This book divides each scenario into several sections, but before we get into the details, I'd like to discuss the most important rule, called the **Golden Rule**. Basically the Golden Rule is that if you, the player, feel that a rule or design feature in any way interferes or hinders with the flow of the game, then feel free to change it. This is not a catch-all for sloppy scenario design. Far from it. The maps have been thoroughly researched and recreated from topographical and historical maps. The Order of Battle has been painstakingly to put together from what records are available. Rather, it is a recognition that not everyone will agree on a rules modification, the strength of a unit on the second day of the battle, or the consolidation of smaller units for ease of game play. If you need to change some rule because you think it will make your game better, then by all means the Golden Rule is for you!

Here is a summary of each section, and how to adapt the set of rules you play to the scenarios.

Background

This is a short background history to put the scenario in context.

Game Overview

This section provides basic information on the game. This includes a brief summary of the number of units and how long the game might take to play. It also includes the size of the game table. The scale for each map is approximately 33 yards per inch. While this might seem unusual, the size and frontage of regiments in most miniature games are too large. Since the majority of players will have their units based on this incorrect frontage, the maps are designed with this in mind, fitting the maps to the actual frontages of the miniatures themselves. Those players that have units based on the correct frontage will still be able to use the maps with little or no modification.

The scenarios are designed for use with 15mm miniatures in mind. For play with 6mm figures, half the ground scale and distances. For 25mm games, double them.

Game turns throughout the book are expressed in brackets. The first digit is the number of turns for 10 minute based games. The second is for 15 minute based games, and the third is for 20 minute based games. So, Turn [7/5/4] would be Turn 7 in a 10 minute based game, Turn 5 in a 15 minute based game, and Turn 4 in a 20 minute based game.

Terrain

The terrain section gives a detailed description of the terrain on the gaming table. It highlights unusual terrain features and any special rules regarding them. There are, however, some universal features that apply to all the maps throughout the book.

Most woods are fairly open with little underbrush. Unless specified in the scenario, woods on the game table should only be one terrain type worse than open for movement. For visibility, they should be the lightest woods possible.

Another important aspect of this scenario book to consider is the movement rates of the units. Units moved a lot faster than most people realized, even through the woods. Most Civil War miniature game rules sets simply move too slowly to replicate, or even have the potential to replicate, the historical outcome. It is therefore highly encouraged to modify the movement rates of the units. While all sets of rules differ, it may not be too difficult to make adjustments. One simple suggestion is to add two inches to all the movement rates. It is simple and easy for everyone to understand. Another suggestion is for those rules that have a split movement rate. There is normal movement, and a chance for additional movement with a die role to see if the unit loses its formation. Consider allowing units to move the entire full movement rate with no penalty. Weapon ranges should not be modified. Again, this increase is just a suggestion, and can be ignored if desired.

The hills in this scenario book vary in size. The standard is 1 inch of elevation per level. However, some scenarios are fought where the terrain was gentler, and the elevations may be only 1/2 inch per level. This will be specified for the scenario. Model hills with gentle slopes where possible, gradually going upward from the base to the summit and not chiseled terraces that block line of sight.

Also, don't be intimidated by the complexity of the hill elevations in this scenario book, especially the scenarios for the assaults on main Vicksburg works. Most people won't be able to customize their terrain to exactly fit the maps. So, if the map calls for a long ridge, and you only have a series of smaller hills, then string them together to make the ridge. Always remember, this is a simulation, not an exact re-creation. And the whole point is to have fun.

Most of the fences on the map are post and rail, or worm fences. Most are easy to climb and take down. Most rules sets provide a penalty for crossing them, usually an inch of movement. There are also clapboard or paling fences on some scenario maps. Lacking horizontal footings for climbing, they provide more of an obstacle to movement and are destroyed upon crossing. In addition, the thin fence boards provide scant protection from musket or canister balls. They do not convey any cover bonuses to a unit stationed behind them. An example is pictured below.

Deployment

This section details the position and deployment of the units that are on the board at the beginning of the game. It also provides the time and place where additional units and reinforcements march onto the board. It then explains any special rules or historical restrictions for the units.

Unless specified in the scenario, brigade command figures should begin the game within an inch of a unit in the brigade. Division command figures begin the game within six inches of any unit it his division. The location of officers above corps command, if any, are written in each scenario.

Victory Conditions

This section highlights how to determine the winner of the scenario. Most of the scenarios involve inflicting more casualties upon your opponent than you take yourself. A few games assign terrain objectives that either needs to be defended or taken by force.

Common to all the scenarios is inflicting casualties on your opponent. Each unit has a Victory Point value. When a player eliminates, captures, or forces an opposing unit off the board they receive the Victory Point value. Victory Point values are:

- 1 Point for each artillery section
- 2 Points for each infantry regiment
- 3 Points for each cavalry regiment
- 3 Points for each mounted infantry regiment
- 3 point for each brigade commander
- 5 points for each division commander
- 7 points for each corps commander
- 10 points for each army commander

So, for example, if a Union player were to rout a Confederate infantry regiment, and that regiment disperses or exits off the end of the game table, the Union player receives 2 Victory Points.

Order of Battle

The Order of Battle section presents the strength of the regiments and batteries used to fight the scenario. Each regiment and battery has several values assigned to it.

↓1 ↓2 ↓3 ↓4 ↓5

3rd Brigade	ES	20	30	40	50	100	Status	Arm.
Col. William Hall [+1]	1,365	68	46	34	27	14		
11th Iowa	260	13	9	7	5	3	3	R
13th Iowa	300	15	10	8	6	3	3	R
15th Iowa	380	19	13	10	8	4	3	R
16th Iowa	425	21	14	11	9	4	3	R

↓6 ↓7 ↓8

Artillery Battalion	ES	Status	Armament
Cpt. Edward Spears Jr. [+1]			
Battery F, 2nd Illinois		3	**6x** 12 lb. N

1. Lists officers, beginning with brigade commanders and upwards. The bonuses they provide to the regiments in their command appear in the bracket. Brigade commander normally have a +1, division commanders a +2, and corps and army commanders +3. Outstanding commanders may have a higher bonus and weaker ones a lower one.
2. Provides the historical strength of the unit at the start of the scenario. ES is Effective Strength. For Confederates, this is the number of men on the firing line. For the Union this would often include the officers as well. Numbers in **black** were taken directly from primary and secondary sources. Numbers in red are derived from simple addition or subtraction. Record keeping rapidly deteriorated during the course of the campaign, and researching the National Archives would not be cost effective. Also, because of the depleted strength of many regiments during the battles of May and June 1864, the scenarios combine many regiments into larger units for ease of play. Because of these factors, most regiment's strengths are, unfortunately, a best guess.
3. This section list the number of miniature figures or stands needed to represent the unit on the game table. Again, this number can be either figures or stands. For example, if your set of rules has a ratio of 1 figure equals 20 soldiers, then you would use the "20" column. If your rules list a ratio of one stand of figures equals 100 soldiers, then you would use the "100" column. Also, feel free to adjust the numbers to fit the way you have your figures based. If your regiments are based in increments of 4 (8, 12, 16), and a regiment is listed as a "15", go ahead and use a 16 figure regiment to represent it.
4. This shows the status or morale of the unit. Values are given as 1, 2, 3, and 4. 1 is for militia and untrained troops and is the lowest value. 2 is for trained units that have seen little or no combat. A value of 3 is your average unit with a few battles and campaigns under their belts. A regiment or battery with a value of 4 has seen numerous battles and has generally prevailed in all of

them. If your set of rules only has three values, then combine some numbers, usually militia and untrained units. In that case, you will only need 2, 3, and 4. Giving each unit a value is a very objective task, though each unit in the battle was researched and an attempt was made to quantify how many engagements they had been in, and how victorious they were in them. As always, follow the Golden Rule. If you disagree with a value for a unit, change it. Also, for simplicity, feel free to assign one value to all the units in a brigade. This can make it easier to keep track of their values during a battle.
5. This column lists the weapons carried by each infantry unit. Some regiments may have used more than one type of firearm by company. In this case, the weapon used by the majority of the regiment is listed. We know what weapons were used by the Union regiments, but the Confederates left almost no record. Weapon types in red are a guess. If the quartermaster for the brigade or division listed smoothbore ammunition in their ordnance, then a few random regiments were assigned muskets.
6. The weapons types are as follows:
    a. R = Rifle-muskets
    b. M = Smoothbore muskets
    c. BR = Breechloading Rifle
    d. C = Muzzle loading Carbines
    e. BC = Breechloading Carbines
    f. RC = Repeating Carbine
    g. RR = Repeating Rifle
7. Some rules allow for an additional officer figure to represent the commander of a battalion of artillery. If the rules played do not, then ignore this entry.
8. This column provides the value for an artillery battery, much the same as for an infantry regiment.
9. This lists the weapon types of an artillery battery. A detailed list of the exact breakdown of each type of weapon in the battery is provided. Players can then adapt that to their chosen rules. Weapon types listed are:
    a. N = 12 lb. Napoleon smoothbore
    b. P = Parrott Rifle
    c. 3" = 3 inch Ordnance Rifle
    d. H = Smoothbore Howitzer
    e. SB = Smoothbore gun
    f. JR = James Rifle[1]
    g. BR = Blakely Rifle
    h. Mtn. H = Mountain Howitzer
    i. 2.25" R = 2.25" Mountain Rifle

[1]There were three types of James Rifles prevalent at the time. Model 1841 6 lb. Guns rifled but maintaining their 3.67" barrel, Model 1841 6 lb. Guns re-bored to 3.80" and then rifled, and newly cast 3.80" rifles that resembled 3" Ordnance Rifles. Unfortunately, all of the 3.80" cannon were designated the same, regardless of the version. For simplicity's sake, I have labelled all three as "6 lb. JR". Would the 3.80" version with the Ordnance profile and longer barrel have had better ballistics? Probably. But without much tedious research to find out exactly which battery had which type, it's not going to make much of a difference on the gaming table.

One note about the units designated as sharpshooters for both sides. They were simply dedicated skirmish units, trained in light infantry tactics. They carried normal infantry rifles, and were not comparable to specifically trained units such as the famed 1st and 2nd US Sharpshooters in the east.

Optional Rules

Most scenarios contain historical restrictions and special rules to accurately play that portion of the battle. If you want to fight the battle in the most historically accurate fashion, and use luck and skill to try and change the outcome, then play the scenario as written. This section provides optional rules for replaying the scenario, more often removing restrictions to allow playing the game with more a free for all feel. For variety, one universal optional rule applies to all the scenarios. The players may disregard the historical placement of regiments within a brigade, and use whatever formation they wish. The location of the brigade itself should not change, but the formation of the regiments within can.

Map

All of the scenarios include two maps. One map shows the units with their starting positions at the beginning of the game, and numbers or letters indicating where new units enter the board. Each tick mark on the sides of the map indicates one foot on the gaming table. There is also a North arrow indicator. The other is a terrain map showing only terrain features. The default map for scenarios is 33 yards per inch map. Since the complete map can get quite cluttered with units on the board, the terrain maps will help with set-up.

A quick word about the maps. The main map is 33 yards per inch as a compromise between several game rules that can vary from 25, 40, to 50 yards per inch. 33 yards per inch also conveniently works out to roughly 1 inch per 100 feet of elevation, which makes map-making easier. Many of the maps cram a lot of action into a small space. While this is historically accurate, it can make for a cramped game. Also, because of the variation between the basing of units in many sets of rules, not all the units on the map may fit in the designated space. For example, one rules set may specify four 1" stands per regiment, while another may use five 1" stands for a unit of the same strength. Obviously, that would throw off the ability to fit every unit in the space allocated on the map. **Use the Golden Rule liberally!** If you are setting up the scenario, and you feel you need more room, adjust the map. Make a 3' x 4' map into a 4' x 5' or 4' x 6' map. Make it work! This is supposed to be fun! Below is a legend for the maps used in this book.

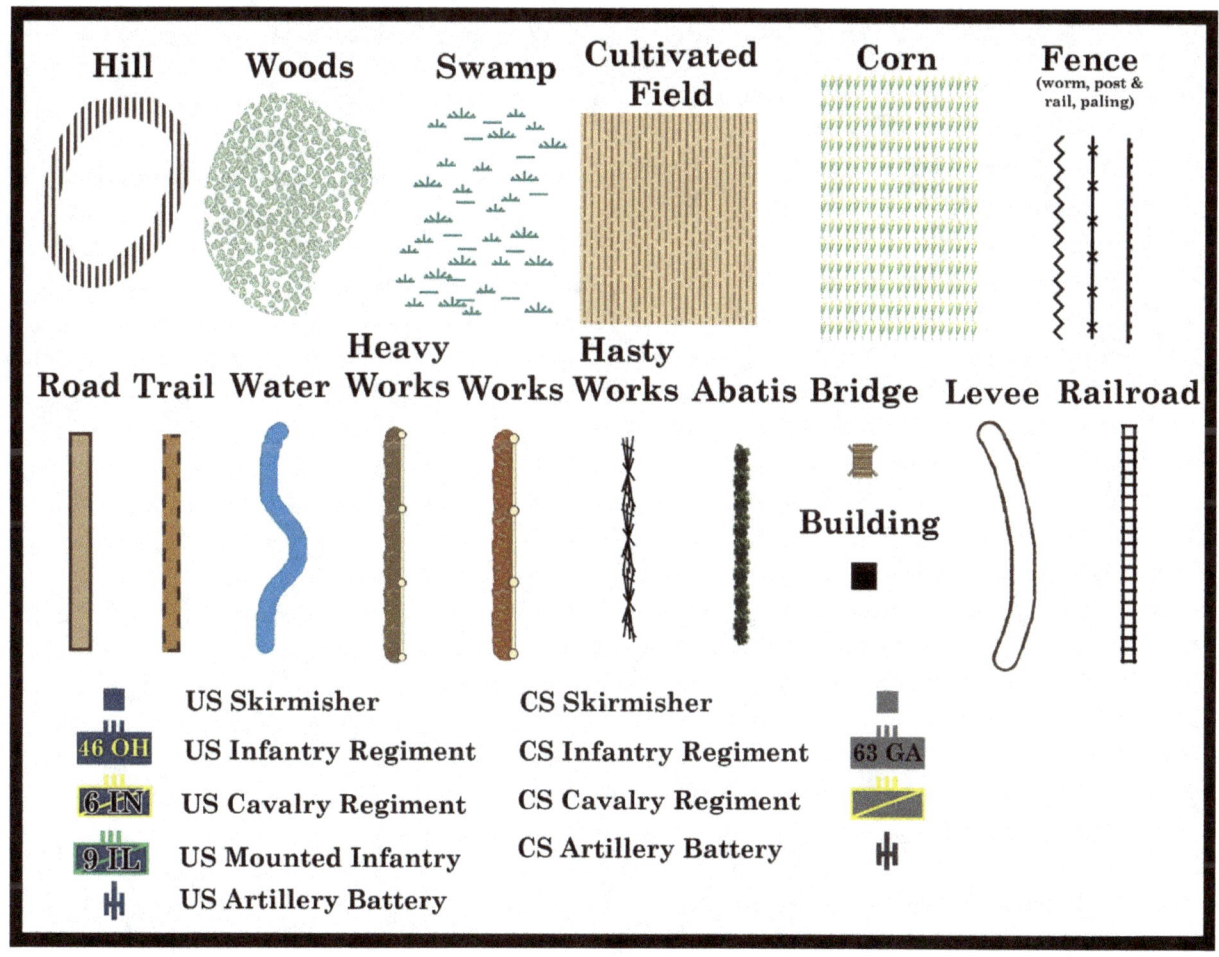

The Battle of Belmont
November 7th, 1861

Background

Early in the American Civil War the Union did not have much of a plan to re-open the Mississippi River. The resources simply were not available, and there were more pressing political and military matters to resolve. One of these was the status of the state of Missouri. Pro-Union and pro-Confederate forces had fought for control of the state and legislature for much of 1861. Battles at Lexington and Wilson Creek ended in the Confederate's favor, but only served to redouble Union efforts to secure the state. Major General John C. Frémont drove the Confederates from Missouri in a relatively bloodless campaign in September and October, 1861, forcing them southward into northern Arkansas.

In early November Frémont learned of Confederate plans to reinforce their armies in northern Arkansas. He ordered Brigadier General Ulysses S. Grant, commander of the District of Southeast Missouri, to put pressure on Columbus, Kentucky to keep the garrison there from sending more men. Columbus was a major fortification commanding the river, with several forts bristling with naval cannon, and thousands of troops. Grant sent two feints towards Columbus. One under Col. Richard Oglesby as a distraction into southeast Missouri, and another commanded by Brigadier General Charles F. Smith into Kentucky.

Grant himself choose to attack Belmont, a small ferry landing and Confederate camp directly across the river from Columbus. On November 6th Grant left Cairo, Illinois with 3,000 men on six transports escorted by two gunboats. They disembarked at Hunter's Farm about three miles north of Belmont at 8 a.m. After getting organized, they marched south towards Belmont. A little after 9 a.m. they encountered Confederates.

When he learned of Grant's movements south by river, the Columbus commander, Major General Leonidas Polk, sent Brigadier General Gideon J. Pillow to reinforce Belmont, although

Brigadier General Ulysses S. Grant

Polk thought Belmont was a feint and the real objective was Columbus itself. Grant and Pillow fought back and forth through the woods north of Belmont for several hours. Both commanders and men were new at this, and it was time to start learning their deadly trade. By the early afternoon the Union gained the upper hand and the Confederate fell back to their camp. The Union made their way through the barricade of fallen trees, and the rebels scattered. Most took shelter below the bluff at the river, and made their way north along the shoreline out of the way.

Once in the rebel camp the Union regiments began looting it and celebrating. Brigadier General John A. McClernand, a politician turned general, even gave rousing speeches. Confederate artillery fire from across the river was ineffective. To restore discipline, Grant ordered the camp burned. Having accomplished his mission, he turned his force around and headed north back towards the waiting transports.

Polk was not sitting on his hands. As the forts at Columbus engaged the Union gunboats, he sent reinforcements of his own across the river. Their arrival turned Grant's march into a gauntlet. The new arrivals joined Pillow's men still available, and almost cut Grant off from his way home. In fact, Grant himself was almost captured when he went looking for an errant regiment and ran into men in grey instead. Ultimately, Grant was the last to board the transports, they found the lost regiments farther north, and the entire force made it back to Cairo intact. Ultimately, the

Confederates considered Belmont a victory, as they had driven off an invader, while Grant felt he had accomplished his strategic objective of keeping Confederate forces in Columbus from reinforcing other rebel armies.

Game Overview

This is a small brigade-on-brigade battle that can easily be played with two players. The field is pretty large for a two brigade battle, but that leaves room to maneuver. It should easily be finished in one gaming session.

The game board is 4'x 6'. The game begins at 9 a.m. and ends when the Union leave the board, either voluntarily or involuntarily.

Terrain

The board is mostly winter woods, with a few roads and fields spread throughout. The southern portion is the Confederate camp at Belmont, and the Mississippi River. The woods only deduct an inch from open movement, but small random clusters of more broken terrain would help give the battlefield a more realistic feel. Visibility is for light woods.

The swampy area to the north is rough terrain, and the water channel is impassable. Fences deduct an inch from movement across them. The plowed fields to not affect the game. The barrier around the Confederate camp, which one Union regimental commander described as "an almost impassable abatis of huge sycamore trees," is rough terrain. The Confederate camps themselves are rough terrain for any unit in line, disorder, or assault columns, but open terrain for skirmish or column as they can weave in and out of the tents and company streets. The bluffs are broken terrain, and should not be very tall. Maybe ½ inch or even ¼. They do provide a cover bonus. The Mississippi River is impassable.

Deployment

Set up the game with the two opposing forces as shown on the scenario map. Grant begins the game next to any of the regiments in the main line, but not with the 27th Illinois or Dollis' cavalry. The Union objective is the capture of the Confederate camps at Belmont. If they can break

Brigadier General Gideon J. Pillow.

through the Confederate line and capture the camps, they must spend one turn completing the destruction of the camps. A unit must be next to one of each of the three camps on the board to destroy it. So it could take only one turn if there is a unit next to all three camps at the same time, or longer if they are destroyed sequentially. Then the Union objective is to escape the battlefield and return to their waiting transports to the north. They must exit the map on the northern edge of the board. Obviously the roads would be quicker, but the fields and woods count too.

Any Union unit that routs still heads towards the northern edge of the board, *if possible* given the specific circumstance. For example, a Confederate charging directly from the north would rout a Federal unit directly south, or back towards Belmont, according to most rules sets. Use common sense when interpreting the rules.

Pillow may begin the game next to any Confederate unit in Russell's Second Brigade. If the Confederates hold the line and prevent the Union from reaching Belmont, it's a Confederate victory. However, if they get pushed back into camp, they can escape below the bluffs or along the road at **1**. The Mississippi River is the edge of the board for any routed Confederate units. Any unit that disperses at the river's edge is out for the rest of the game.

Many of the Confederate units have substandard flintlock muskets. Make sure to take those into account when playing the game.

If the Union makes it to the camps at Belmont, General Polk will send reinforcements. The brigades under Cheatham/Smith and Walker arrive at **2** one hour, or [7/5/4] Turns, after the first Union unit breaches the abatis. Any unit that escaped along the roads or bluffs may rejoin and enter one turn afterwards. They are at the same morale as when they left, and suffer the same penalties for loss of stands/figures previously taken as casualties. The Confederate objective is to trap or remove as many Union units as possible before they escape off the board.

Victory Conditions

Who won in the game is decided by Victory Points. At the end of the game, award Victory Points for the enemy units removed from the game. The side with the most points wins. The exception is if the Confederates win the initial battle in the woods and the Union never reaches Belmont. That is an automatic Confederate victory, and possibly the end of Grant's career.

The Confederates have the greatest chance of victory by holding off the Union at the very beginning, or engaging the Union as they march back to the transports and routing/forcing them into towards Belmont for certain capture. The Union must rely on good tactics and speed to overcome the first rebel line, burn the camps quickly, and return just as fast.

Order of Battle

District of Southeast Missouri

BG Ulysses S. Grant [+2]

McClernand's Brigade	ES	20	30	40	50	100	Status	Arm.
BG John A. McClernand [+1]	1,830	92	61	46	37	18		
27th Illinois	720	36	24	18	14	7	2	M
30th Illinois	500	25	17	13	10	5	2	R
31st Illinois	610	31	20	15	12	6	2	M

Dougherty's Brigade	ES	20	30	40	50	100	Status	Arm.
Col. Henry Dougherty [+1]	837	42	28	21	17	8		
7th Iowa	410	21	14	10	8	4	2	M
22nd Illinois	427	21	14	11	9	4	2	M

Cavalry	ES	20	30	40	50	100	Status	Arm.
Dollis & Delano Cavalry Cos.	128	6	4	3	3	1	2	C

Artillery	ES	Status	Armament
Battery B, 1st Illinois	114	2	**4x** 6 lb. SB, **2x** 12 lb. H

Western Department

First Division
BG Gideon J. Pillow [+1]

First Brigade	ES	20	30	40	50	100	Status	Arm.
Col. J. Knox Walker [+0]	1,493	75	50	37	30	15		
11th Louisiana*	495	25	17	12	10	5	2	M
2nd Tennessee	521	26	17	13	10	5	2	M(F)
15th Tennessee	477	24	16	12	10	5	2	M(F)

*Attached from Third Division

Second Brigade	ES	20	30	40	50	100	Status	Arm.
Col. Robert M. Russell [+1]	2,500	125	83	63	50	25		
13th Arkansas*	553	28	18	14	11	6	2	M
12th Tennessee	485	24	16	12	10	5	2	M
13th Tennessee	472	24	16	12	9	5	2	M(F)
21st Tennessee	466	23	16	12	9	5	2	M
22nd Tennessee	524	26	17	13	10	5	2	M(F)

*Attached from Third Division

Unassigned	ES	20	30	40	50	100	Status	Arm.
1st Mississippi Cavalry Bn.	186	9	6	5	4	2	2	Sh

Artillery	ES	Status	Armament
Watson's Louisiana Battery		2	**4x** 6 lb. SB, **2x** 12 lb. H

Second Division
BG Benjamin F. Cheatham [+1]

First Brigade	ES	20	30	40	50	100	Status	Arm.
Col. Preston Smith [+1]	919	46	31	23	18	9		
1st Mississippi Bn.	362	18	12	9	7	4	2	M
154th Tennessee	557	28	19	14	11	6	2	R

Optional Rules

The green Union troops began looting the Confederate camps when they captured them, and General McClernand didn't do much to stop them. Only when Grant ordered the camps burned did some semblance of order return. If you wish to replicate this, have any Union regiment that gets within an inch of a Confederate camp go into disorder and loot the camp. They will remain there until General Grant arrives within the rule's command radius, at which point the regiments can begin destroying the camps per the scenario conditions. Only Grant can stop the looting.

Author's Notes

This is a good early war battle, with a few extra conditions as the Union must also burn the Confederate camps and escape. All the while, both sides are green and often has substandard early war weapons.

The modern battlefield has virtually nothing left of the woods or terrain features, and is all on private property. Therefore I decided not to take the trip there to take pictures. However, there is a park on the Columbus side with some of the fortifications still available to visit.

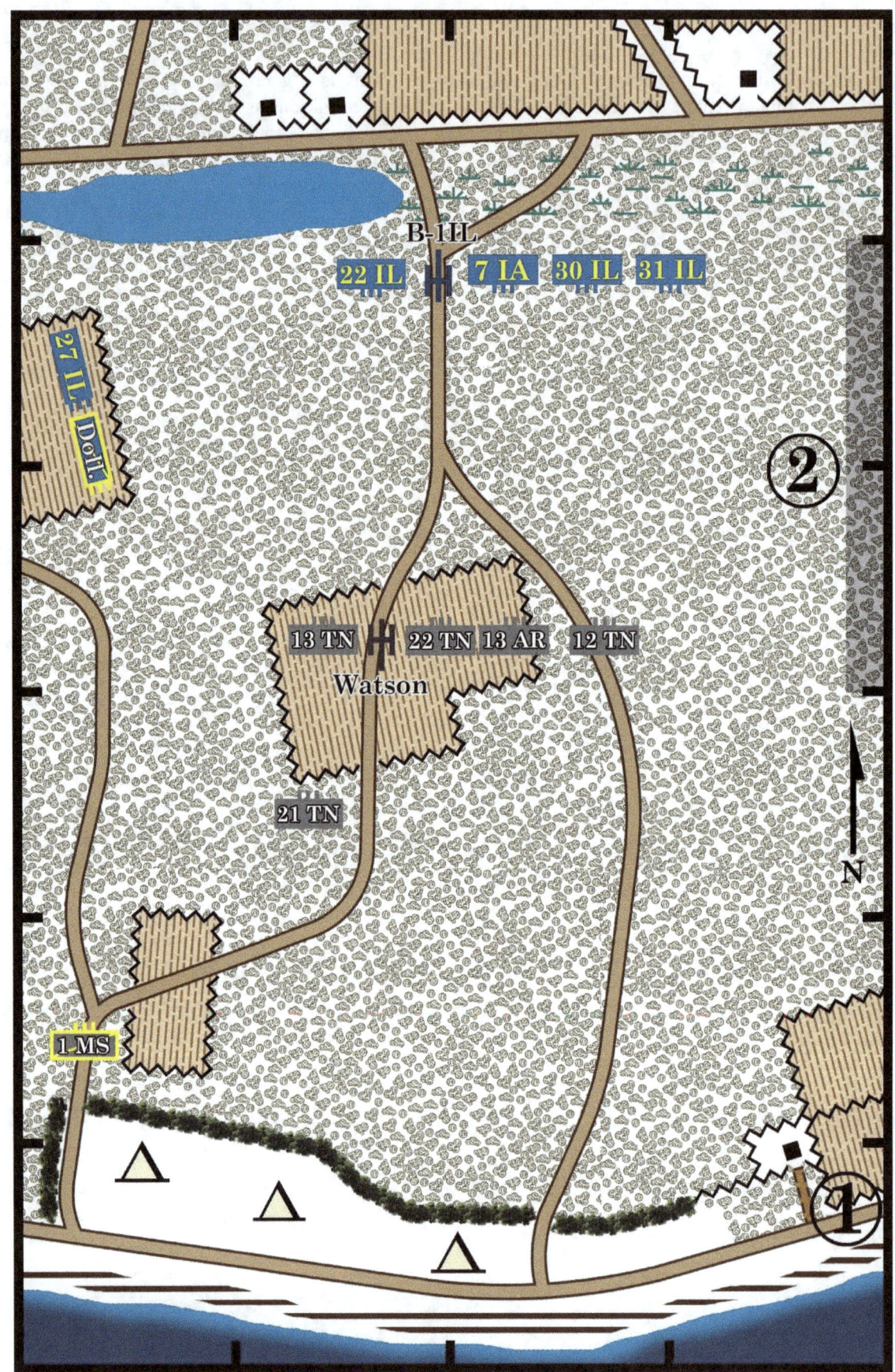

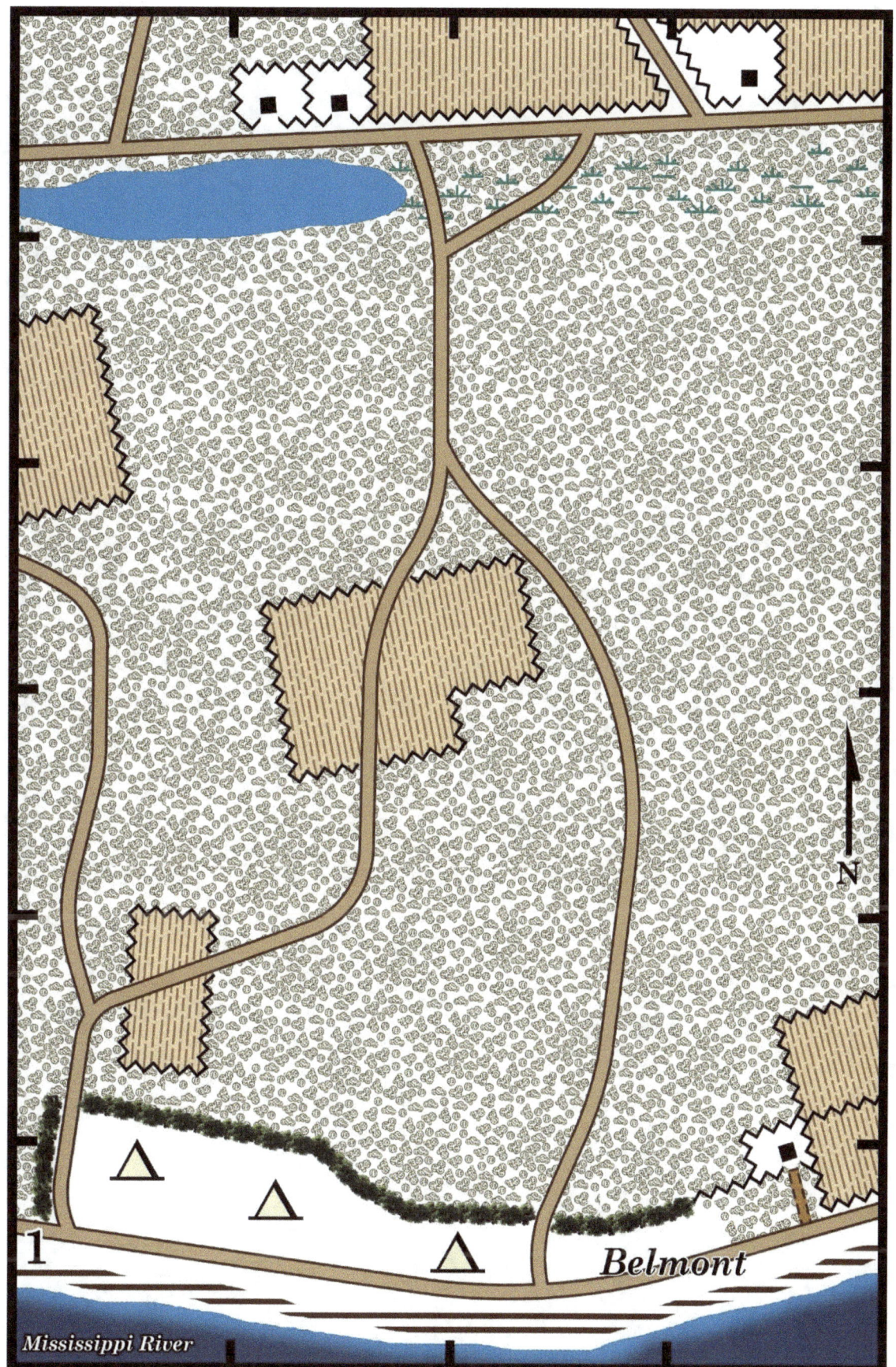

The Battle of Baton Rouge
August 5th, 1862

Background

In April 1862 the drive to retake the Mississippi River began in earnest. Union Admiral David G. Farragut stormed up the mouth of the river past the defending forts, and captured New Orleans on April 25th. Continuing up the river, a naval landing party captured the town and the pre-war fort and arsenal there. From there Farragut continued north, but was unsuccessful in capturing Vicksburg.

Major General Earl Van Dorn, commanding Confederate forces in Mississippi at the time, determined to liberate Baton Rouge. From there they could attack Union garrisons along the Red River, and eventually retake New Orleans. On July 27th he dispatched Major General John C. Breckinridge and his division from Vicksburg to Baton Rouge. He was joined outside of Baton Rouge by another small division led by Brigadier General Daniel Ruggles. The small corps arrived outside of Baton Rouge after midnight in the early morning of August 5th. Also heading south was the Confederate ironclad ram *C.S.S. Arkansas*. As Breckinridge was attacking, the *Arkansas* was to destroy the Union fleet anchored at the town.

Baton Rouge was defended by an oversized brigade commanded by Brigadier General Thomas R. Williams. Williams knew of Breckinridge's approach, but not when he would arrive. Most of his brigade was camped in the eastern fringes of the town, which was not as developed and scattered with woodlots and open fields. When the Union pickets opened fire at the arriving Confederates in the dark, the rebel's element of surprise was lost.

The Union quickly formed in the dark, but fog kept visibility low. The 21st Indiana Infantry and 6th Massachusetts Battery moved eastward towards the very edge of town, but encountered the approaching Confederates in the lightening twilight. The two sides traded fire in the fog, but the Union wisely fell back. At about 4:30 a.m. the battle began in full. A small flanking force under Lt. Colonel Thomas Shields of the 30th Louisiana

Brigadier General Thomas R. Williams

routed the 14th Maine from their camp, using the fog to exaggerate their numbers. The battle then waged back and forth along the streets and wood lots of the town.

At about 10 a.m. General Williams led the 21st Indiana in a charge to regain their camp. He was "shot dead off his horse," according to one eyewitness. Colonel Thomas W. Cahill of the 9th Connecticut took over. He quickly ordered a retreat back into the town to prepared fortifications, and under the powerful guns of the Union gunboats in the river. According to Cahill, Williams had discussed this plan with him shortly before his death.

As the Federals left Breckinridge paused to regroup. He knew the Union were now in a powerful position, behind works and defended by the gunboats. The *Arkansas* had not arrive to attack the Union fleet. Unknown to the Breckinridge, the *Arkansas* developed engine trouble and did not attack. Reluctantly, Breckinridge decided to call off the attack and retire. There was no way he was going to prevail against the firepower of the Union navy.

Game Overview

This is a small division sized battle in a unique setting, the middle of an urban area. The number of units on each side is about even.

The game begins at dawn at 4:30 a.m. and ends at 10 a.m., or earlier if the Union are driven off the board.

The modern Baton Rouge cemetery looking east. Much fighting occurred back and forth across the cemetery grounds.

Terrain

The game terrain is flat except for a gully in the northwest corner. For convenience, it's OK to remove that feature and simply have the creek there for an easier set up. Die hard gamers may still want to put it there for accuracy's sake.

Most sources show this eastern part of town was not as built up as it was closer to the river. There are no existing maps of the building layout, so players should fill in the lots with random scatterings of home and urban fences. In fact, there could be *fewer* homes on the east, or right, side of the map. So feel free to remove some if desired. The orphanage, however, was located in the spot indicated. Obviously this layout will take a lot of road terrain pieces. Just do the best you can.

Fences cost an inch of movement. The creek is rough terrain, and if on the map, the slopes of the gully are broken terrain. The woods on the map are open woods, most of the underbrush having been gathered and used for firewood. In fact, many of the fences had as well, so showing gaps or swaths of empty fences near the Union camps would be accurate too. The woods only deduct an inch of movement, and visibility is clear for the first six inches. After that roll for visibility as light woods.

The camps themselves are rough terrain for any unit in line, disorder, or assault columns, but open terrain for skirmish or column. The cornfield blocks line of sight for any unit on the outside looking in. If both units are inside the cornfield, they can roll for visibility as if they are in heavy woods. The cemetery does not affect movement or cover.

The morning fog is the big limiter of visibility during the game. Roll for visibility like light woods. If in the actual woods, roll for both. Roll for the fog first. If you can see past the first six inches of the woods, roll for the woods visibility. Whichever additional distance is shorter is the maximum visibility of the unit. Also because of the fog, a unit may not charge another unit unless they had a line of sight to the unit the previous turn. Different rules handle turn sequences differently, so it may be possible that an attacking unit saw a target the previous turn, but lost line of sight on the current turn. They could still charge, but it may not turn out the way they expected. But such is war. The main goal is to avoid unrealistically charging a unit the player can see,

Major General John C. Breckinridge

but the unit could not. The fog lifts at 8 a.m., or Turn [22/15/11].

Deployment

Begin the battle with the regiments and batteries in position as shown. The initial position of the 21st Indiana Infantry (actually their second, fallback position) is different between reports and maps. The regiment can be deployed in either position shown. Although the maps in the Official Records favor the solid one, modern historians favor the alternative. Williams begins the game at the orphanage. The 4th Wisconsin, 9th Connecticut, and 4th Massachusetts Battery arrive on the road at **1** on Turn [16/11/8].

The 21st Indiana and 6th Massachusetts Battery have already been fighting, so they do not get an opening or initial volley benefit.

For the Confederates, Breckinridge enters the board at **2** on Turn [2/2/2]. The batteries of Hudson, Cobb, and the remainder of Semmes arrive at **3** on Turn [10/7/5].

The 3rd and 6th Kentucky also do not get an opening or initial volley benefit.

Victory Conditions

The game ends if the Union forces are forced off the board, or the 10 a.m. Turn [34/23/17], whichever comes first. If the Union remain on the board at the end of the game, they fall back to the fortifications closer to the river under the protection of the Union gunboats, and win the game. If the Confederates force the Union off before the end, it is a Confederate victory.

Order of Battle

Department of the Gulf

2nd Brigade
BG Thomas R. Williams [+1]*

*Commands the Baton Rouge garrison as well. Can provide a benefit to any Union unit in the battle.

2nd Brigade, Right Wing Col. Nathan A. M. Dudley [+0]	ES	20	30	40	50	100	Status	Arm.
	1,175	59	39	29	24	12		
30th Massachusetts	350	18	12	9	7	4	2	R
6th Michigan	600	30	20	15	12	6	2	R
7th Vermont	225	11	8	6	5	2	2	R

Artillery Battalion*	ES	Status	Armament
Indiana Battery (21st)		2	**3x** 6 lb. SB
2nd Massachusetts Battery		2	**6x** 6 lb. JR
4th Massachusetts Battery		2	**4x** 6 lb. JR, **2x** 12 lb. H
6th Massachusetts Battery		2	**4x** 12 lb. N, **2x** 6 lb. JR

*Under the command of Col. Dudley

Looking from the eastern edge of the cornfield to the west. This land lot was part of the cemetery in 1862, but was empty and planted with corn instead.

2nd Brigade, Left Wing	ES	20	30	40	50	100	Status	Arm.
Col. Frank S. Nickerson [+0]	1,836	92	61	46	37	18		
9th Connecticut	200	10	7	5	4	2	2	R
21st Indiana	536	27	18	13	11	5	2	R
14th Maine	800	40	27	20	16	8	2	R
4th Wisconsin	300	15	10	8	6	3	2	R

Breckinridge's Corps
MG John C. Breckinridge [+2]

First Division
BG Charles Clark [+2]

Second Brigade	ES	20	30	40	50	100	Status	Arm.
Col. Thomas H. Hunt [+0]	908	45	30	23	18	9		
31st Alabama, 4th Alabama Bn.	281	14	9	7	6	3	3	R
31st Mississippi	325	16	11	8	7	3	2	R
4th, 5th Kentucky	302	15	10	8	6	3	3	R

	ES	Status	Armament
Hudson's Mississippi Battery		2	**2x** 6 lb. SB, **2x** 12 lb. H

Fourth Brigade	ES	20	30	40	50	100	Status	Arm.
Col. Thomas B. Smith [+1]	391	20	13	10	8	4		
Smith	391	20	13	10	8	4	3	M

	ES	Status	Armament
Cobb's Kentucky Battery		3	**3x** 6 lb. SB

Second Division
BG Daniel Ruggles [+2]

First Brigade	ES	20	30	40	50	100	Status	Arm.
Col. Albert P. Thompson [+]	916	46	31	23	18	9		
3rd Kentucky, 35th Alabama	472	24	16	12	9	5	3	M
6th, 7th Kentucky, Sharpshooter Co.	444	22	15	11	9	4	3	R

Fourth Brigade	ES	20	30	40	50	100	Status	Arm.
Col. Henry W. Allen [+]	945	47	32	24	19	9		
4th Louisiana, 39th Mississippi Co. I	400	20	13	10	8	4	3	M
30th Louisiana, 9th Louisiana Bn.	395	20	13	10	8	4	2	R
Shield's Detachment	150	8	5	4	3	2	2	R

	ES	Status	Armament
Semmes' Battery	89	2	**4x** 6 lb. SB, **2x** 6 lb. JR

Optional Rules

There are no optional rules for this game, other than the alternate placement of the 21st Indiana.

Author's Notes

Urban combat was rare during the Civil War. The only other infantry example that comes to mind is Barksdale's defense of downtown Fredericksburg, and a few cavalry raids. It makes for an unusual game that could be a welcome break from the usual open fields and woods.

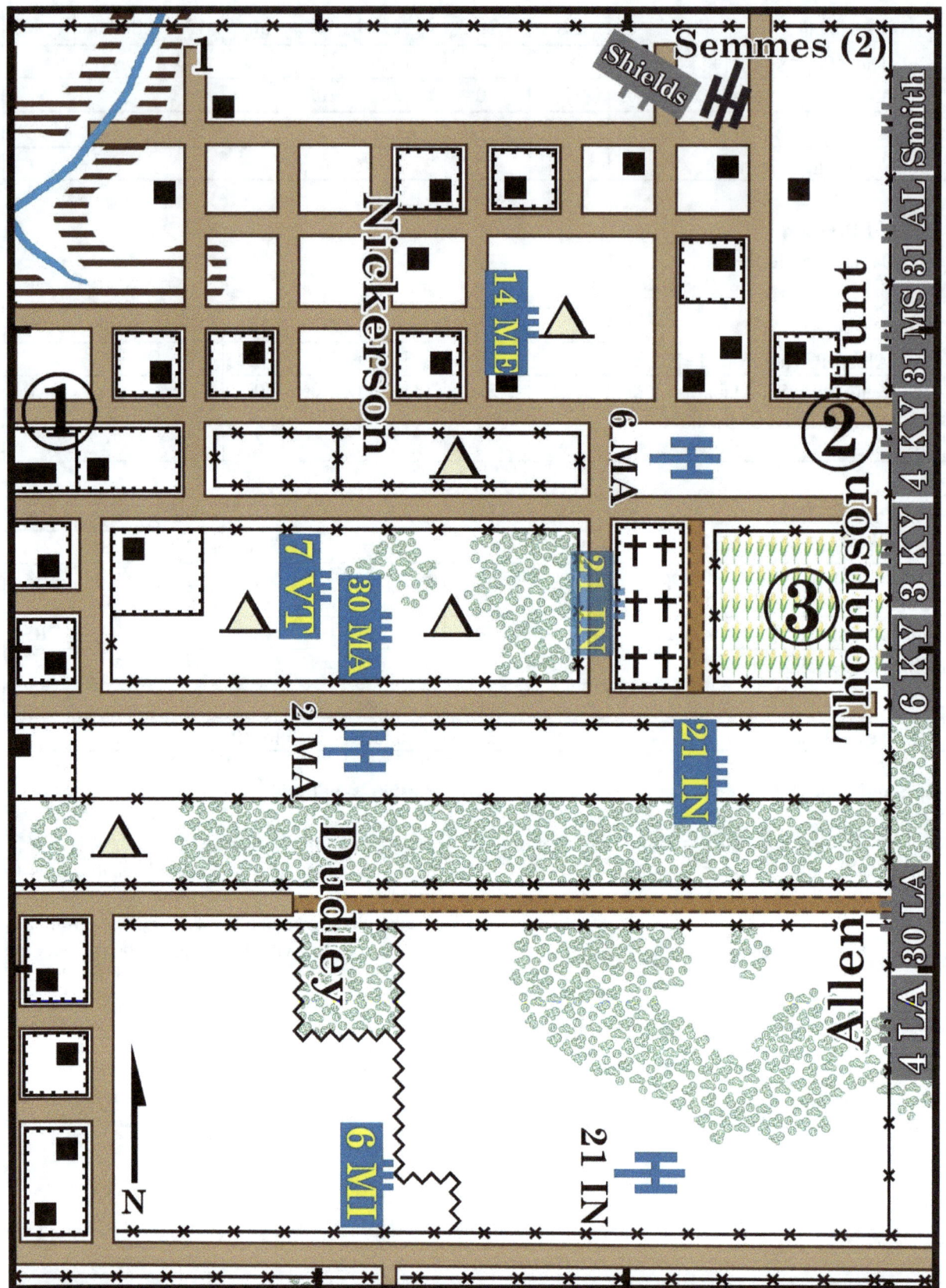

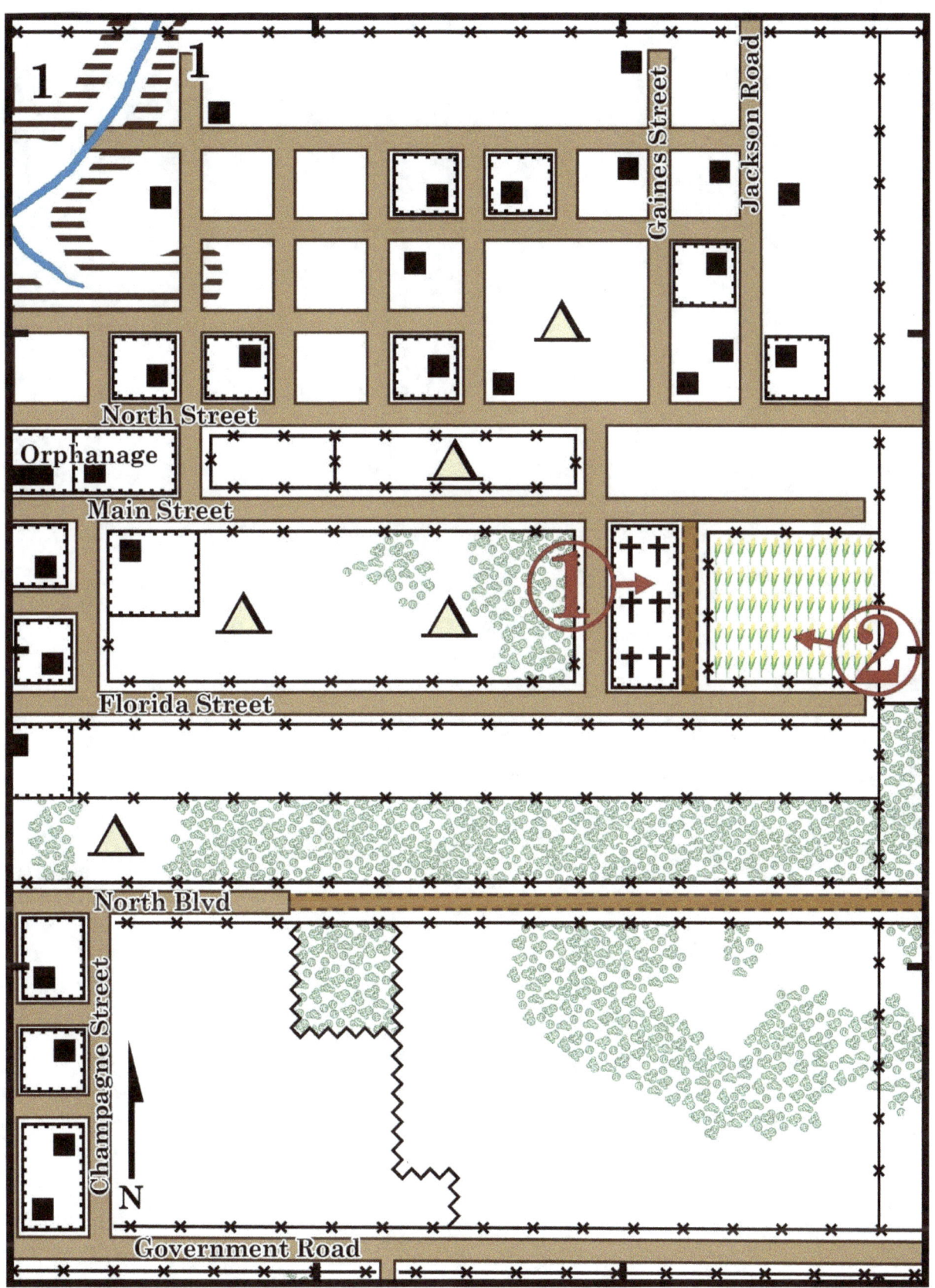

The Battle of Chickasaw Bayou
December 29th, 1862

Background

The campaign to capture Vicksburg, Mississippi began in October 1862. Vicksburg was the linchpin of the Confederate river defenses. Located on high bluffs on a hair pin turn of the river, its numerous and well-armed batteries commanded the river traffic below. The countryside to the north was a myriad of rivers and swamps, making approach from that direction difficult without swinging wide to the east nearer the state capital of Jackson. Not to mention the distance required to campaign overland from the northern reaches of the state.

Union Major General Ulysses S. Grant had a formidable army in his Department of the Tennessee located in northern Mississippi. He would need it, as approaching Vicksburg would be difficult. To get ready for his planned campaign, he pulled together every last soldier he could from outlying districts and concentrated his army. In addition, he called for more reinforcements. One source was a recruitment drive in Illinois being undertaken by one of his subordinates, Major General John A. McClernand. McClernand had been promised an independent command by the Lincoln administration, if he could recruit it. McClernand sent thousands of new recruits south to Memphis, where he expected to join "his" men and lead them in an assault on Vicksburg. In a deft sleight of hand, Grant took command of these men, by virtue of their presence in his department, and gave command of them to Major General William T. Sherman. Before a livid McClernand understood what was happening, Grant sent Sherman south by transport along the Mississippi River to attack Vicksburg. At the same time, Grant was in the midst of his own overland campaign through the middle of the state.

After a brief stop at Helena, Arkansas to pick up even more men, Sherman arrived north of the city on Christmas Eve, December 24th. On December 26th, he began unloading men at Walter Johnson's plantation on the Yazoo River, a tributary of the Mississippi. Soon Sherman's

Major General William T. Sherman

entire army was disembarking. The Confederates reacted quickly, sending men and artillery to slow him down. The terrain heavily favored the rebels. Sherman had landed on a wide river plain that extended eastward toward a series of high bluffs known as the Walnut Hills. At the base of the hills was a major roadway knows as the Valley Road. Intertwined along the river plain were a series of sluggish creeks and streams called bayous in the southeastern United States. However, any waterway throughout Louisiana and Mississippi were often labelled as a bayou regardless of whether it was "sluggish" or not. In Sherman's case, these brackish waterways were generally impassable, causing major headaches as the Confederates skirmished and contested his advance at every major crossing point.

By the evening of December 28th he had pushed the Confederates back to the last series of bayous at the base of the Walnut Hills. Here was the rebel main line of defense. Chickasaw Bayou generally paralleled the Valley Road to the south. It was too deep to cross except at very few points, and each side of the bayou had steep levees, with the southern, or Confederate banks being measurably higher and commanding the opposite side. The Southern commander on site, Brigadier General Stephen D. Lee, placed his men well. Instead of fortifying the hills themselves, he built a line of defenses at their base covering the only crossing points over Chickasaw Bayou. One was a trail over a small sand spit, and others guarded the main roads from the Johnson and Annie Lake plantations.

The view down what was then Lake Plantation Road towards the Confederate line. This is roughly the location of the corduroy ford. This area would have been plowed fields all the way to the Valley Road in the distance.

Sherman decided to focus his main efforts on December 29th on the Lake plantation road, with a secondary effort on the trail over the sand spit. To provide a diversion, and possibly develop into something further, he tasked a group of pioneers to build a pontoon bridge in the woods between them. The terrain was his greatest enemy, as even approaching these crossing points was difficult. The woods were a series of smaller waterways, brambles, and underbrush, and only the road and trails allowed for quick movement.

The morning began with Brigadier General Andrew J. Smith's Second Division attacking through the sand spit. The 6th Missouri (Union) Infantry managed to gain a foothold at the base of the Confederate levee on the southern side, but could make no more headway. The Confederates had turned the levee into a strong earthwork, with supporting artillery fire from the rear. Even with more regiments lining the banks to provide covering fire, the narrow crossing proved impossible to capture or exploit.

The effort to construct the pontoon bridge to their left failed as well. The Confederate skirmishers were too well dug in on the opposite levee to dislodge, and inflicted too many casualties on the pioneers to continue their work safely.

The main effort was along the Lake Plantation Road, and here Lee had set a deadly trap. He didn't fortify the crossing itself, a relatively good crossing with a corduroyed wood ford. Instead, Lee built his defenses in a semi-circle around the ford. As Brigadier General George W. Morgan's division crossed, they met fire from three directions. The lead brigade was devastated, and reinforcement only added to the casualty lists. Brigadier General Francis P. Blair, Jr's brigade moved through the dense woods and bayous to outflank the crossing, but the effort took too long to help, and the rebel defenses inflicted considerable losses to him as well. Sherman simply could not bring his superior numbers to bear over the limited crossings available over Chickasaw Bayou, and he called off the assault.

With his failure to advance, and the ever increasing reinforcements arriving for the Confederates, Sherman recognized that his thrust had been blunted. To the north, Grant's campaign ended in disaster when a rebel cavalry raid destroyed his supply base at Holly Springs, and another cavalry raid in western Tennessee significantly damaged his railroad lifeline to the north. Grant was forced back into the northern reaches of Mississippi. Sherman reloaded his

Brigadier General Stephen D. Lee

transports on January 2nd, 1863 and retired back north.

Game Overview

This is a division-sized game. One Confederate player could probably handle all forces available, while 2-4 could play the Union. The Union will be fighting the terrain as much as the Confederates.

The game table is 4' x 6'. The game starts at 11:30 a.m. and ends when the Confederates are pushed off the board, or the Union can no longer advance.

Terrain

Most of the map is flat, level terrain, except for the Walnut Hills that rise abruptly on the other side of the Valley Road. The hills are steep and should be 1" for each elevation. The Indian Mound should be just large enough to fit a section of artillery and the medium works lunette around it. It should be able to look directly down the trail and ford at the sand spit. The light colored woods are open woods that only deducts an inch from movement. Visibility is for light woods. The darker colored forest is broken terrain, and heavy woods for visibility. This is probably a bit better than the historic terrain, but ease of game play takes precedence. The plowed fields do not affect the game.

The dark colored water obstacles, such as the top half of Chickasaw Bayou and Fishing Lake, are impassable. The light colored portion of Chickasaw Bayou and the bayou behind Sheldon's brigade, are rough terrain. The streams on the Confederate side of the bayous are broken terrain, and provide a small cover bonus to any unit using them for protection. The corduroy ford and the darker branch of Chickasaw Bayou crossing the Lake Plantation Road deduct an inch from movement. The ford at the sand spit subtracts deduct two inches. These fords can only be crossed in march column or disorder. The fords over the smaller streams on the Valley Road do not have any movement penalties

The bayous have levees on each side to control flooding. The ones on the Confederate side are taller. To be accurate, you could have the Confederate ones be ½" tall and the Union side ¼" tall. The taller Confederates ones act as medium works, the Union side as light or hasty works. This applies to both sides. So for example, if a Union unit gets to the southern side and uses the levee as cover from the artillery section on the Indian Mound, they get to use the levee as medium works. The openings in the levee for the trail over the sand spit should only be wide enough to fit a trail through it.

Deployment

Start the game set up as shown. Blair's brigade is split in two. The two regiments guarding and supporting the artillery can only be controlled by their division commander Brigadier General Frederick Steele, or Sherman. There should be one stand of pioneers, numbering about 100-120 men, at the point on the map. They are always considered to be in skirmish formation. If they spend four turns building the pontoon bridge, they will successfully complete it. They do not have to be consecutive turns. So they can fall back and return if necessary. They are in the middle of construction when the 42nd Georgia arrives to stop them.

Reinforcement arrive on Turn [8/6/5]. Thayer's brigade enters at **1** and Hovey's brigade at **2**. Both are in double line of battle. General Steele enters on the Lake Plantation Road. Sherman arrives on the Lake Plantation Road on Turn [13/9/7].

The Confederates are in position to defend the crossings. General Lee begins the game with his own brigade. The left of the 31st Louisiana should extend over the trail to block unrestricted travel over the sand spit. The rest of the regiment is on the levee. Reinforcements are on the way from Barton's brigade.

Co. I, 1st Mississippi Artillery rides onto the board at **3** on the Valley Road on Turn [8/6/5]. The 4th Mississippi, 46th Mississippi, and 22nd Louisiana arrive on Turn [14/10/8]. They enter the board at **3** in march column.

Victory Conditions

The game ends when the Confederates have been forced off the board, or the Union can no longer advance.

Order of Battle

Army of the Tennessee

Thirteenth Army Corps
MG William T. Sherman [+2]

2nd Division
BG Andrew J. Smith [+2]*
*In temporary command.

1st Brigade	ES	20	30	40	50	100	Status	Arm.
Col. Giles A. Smith [+1]	2,360	118	79	59	47	24		
113th Illinois	584	29	19	15	12	6	2	R
116th Illinois	602	30	20	15	12	6	2	R
6th Missouri	421	21	14	11	8	4	3	R
8th Missouri	388	19	13	10	8	4	3	R
13th United States, 1st Bn.	365	18	12	9	7	4	2	R

4th Brigade	ES	20	30	40	50	100	Status	Arm.
Col. T. Kilby Smith [+0]	1,758	88	59	44	35	18		
55th Illinois	346	17	12	9	7	3	3	R
83rd Indiana	641	32	21	16	13	6	2	R
54th Ohio	412	21	14	10	8	4	3	R
57th Ohio	359	18	12	9	7	4	3	R

3rd Division
BG George W. Morgan [+2]

1st Brigade	ES	20	30	40	50	100	Status	Arm.
Col. Lionel A. Sheldon [+1]	1,672	84	56	42	33	17		
118th Illinois	457	23	15	11	9	5	2	R
69th Indiana	571	29	19	14	11	6	3	R
120th Ohio	644	32	21	16	13	6	2	R

The Valley Road. The intersection with the Lake Plantation Road is just ahead. The view is looking southwest towards Vicksburg.

2nd Brigade	ES	20	30	40	50	100	Status	Arm.
Col. Daniel W. Lindsey [+1]	1,849	92	62	46	37	18		
49th Indiana	566	28	19	14	11	6	2	R
7th Kentucky	599	30	20	15	12	6	3	R
114th Ohio	684	34	23	17	14	7	2	R

3rd Brigade	ES	20	30	40	50	100	Status	Arm.
Col. John F. DeCourcy [+1]	2,543	127	85	64	51	25		
54th Indiana	659	33	22	16	13	7	2	R
22nd Kentucky	445	22	15	11	9	4	2	R
16th Ohio	848	42	28	21	17	8	3	M
42nd Ohio	591	30	20	15	12	6	3	R

Artillery	ES	Status	Armament
Battery G, 1st Michigan		3	**6x** 3" R
1st Wisconsin Battery		3	**4x** 20 lb. P

	ES	20	30	40	50	100	Status	Arm.
Pioneers	120	6	4	3	2	1		
Pioneers	120	6	4	3	2	1	3	R

4th Division
BG Frederick Steele [+2]

1st Brigade	ES	20	30	40	50	100	Status	Arm.
BG Francis P. Blair, Jr. [+1]	3,233	162	108	81	65	32		
13th Illinois	521	26	17	13	10	5	2	R
29th Missouri	602	30	20	15	12	6	2	R
30th Missouri	536	27	18	13	11	5	2	R
31st Missouri	551	28	18	14	11	6	2	R
32nd Missouri	597	30	20	15	12	6	2	R
58th Ohio	426	21	14	11	9	4	3	R

Artillery	ES	Status	Armament
4th Ohio Battery		3	**4x** 6 lb. JR, **2x** 12 lb. H

2nd Brigade	ES	20	30	40	50	100	Status	Arm.
BG Charles E. Hovey [+1]	2,993	150	100	75	60	30		
25th Iowa	562	28	19	14	11	6	2	R
31st Iowa	502	25	17	13	10	5	2	R
3rd Missouri	445	22	15	11	9	4	3	R
12th Missouri	511	26	17	13	10	5	3	R
17th Missouri	496	25	17	12	10	5	3	R
76th Ohio	477	24	16	12	10	5	3	R

4th Brigade	ES	20	30	40	50	100	Status	Arm.
BG John M. Thayer [+1]	2,748	137	92	69	55	27		
4th Iowa	480	24	16	12	10	5	3	R
9th Iowa	531	27	18	13	11	5	3	R
26th Iowa	544	27	18	14	11	5	2	R
30th Iowa	578	29	19	14	12	6	2	R
34th Iowa	615	31	21	15	12	6	2	R

Corps Artillery	ES	Status	Armament
Battery A, 1st Illinois		3	**4x** 6 lb. SB, **2x** 12 lb. H
Battery B, 1st Illinois		3	**5x** 6 lb. SB, **1x** 12 lb. H

Department of Mississippi and East Louisiana

Second Military District
BG Stephen D. Lee [+2]*
*Commands his large brigade and all the forces on the field.

Barton's Brigade	ES	20	30	40	50	100	Status	Arm.
BG Seth Barton [+1]	1,650	83	55	41	33	17		
40th Georgia	386	19	13	10	8	4	2	R
42nd Georgia	478	24	16	12	10	5	2	R
43rd Georgia	405	20	14	10	8	4	2	R
52nd Georgia	381	19	13	10	8	4	2	R

Vaughn's Brigade	ES	20	30	40	50	100	Status	Arm.
BG John C. Vaughn [+1]	1,205	60	40	30	24	12		
60th Tennessee	584	29	19	15	12	6	2	M
62nd Tennessee	621	31	21	16	12	6	2	R

Lee's Command	ES	20	30	40	50	100	Status	Arm.
BG Stephen D. Lee [+2]	4,267	213	142	107	85	43		
17th Louisiana	485	24	16	12	10	5	3	R
22nd Louisiana	179	9	6	4	4	2	2	M
26th Louisiana	572	29	19	14	11	6	2	R
29th Louisiana[a]	605	30	20	15	12	6	2	M
31st Louisiana	567	28	19	14	11	6	2	M
4th Mississippi	508	25	17	13	10	5	3	R
46th Mississippi	504	25	17	13	10	5	2	R
3rd Tennessee[b]	401	20	13	10	8	4	3	R
30th Tennessee[b]	446	22	15	11	9	4	3	R

Artillery	ES	Status	Armament
Co. A, 1st Mississippi Artillery		3	**2x** 12 lb. N
Co. D, 1st Mississippi Artillery		3	**2x** 6 lb. SB, **2x** 12 lb. H
Co. E, 1st Mississippi Artillery		3	**4x** 10 lb. P
Co. I, 1st Mississippi Artillery		3	**2x** 6 lb. SB

[a] Also sometimes known as the 28th Louisiana.
[b] Attached from Brigadier General John Gregg's Brigade.

A wartime sketch of a Union position along a bayou after the battle. Most likely Fishing Lake.

Optional Rules

There are no optional rules for this scenario.

Author's Notes

This is a tough game for the Union. It's more of a study on solving the tactical problem of the limited approaches than a straight up wargame. As such, it might not appeal to many players. However, if you enjoy a challenge, and figuring out how to do better than Sherman, this might be the game for you.

For this and the subsequent battles in this book, I obtained the Union regimental monthly returns. By adding or subtracting casualties reasonable regimental strengths have been calculated for the scenarios. Perhaps not as accurate as a number straight from the Official Records, or the morning muster reports for a specific day, but it's closer than a wild guess.

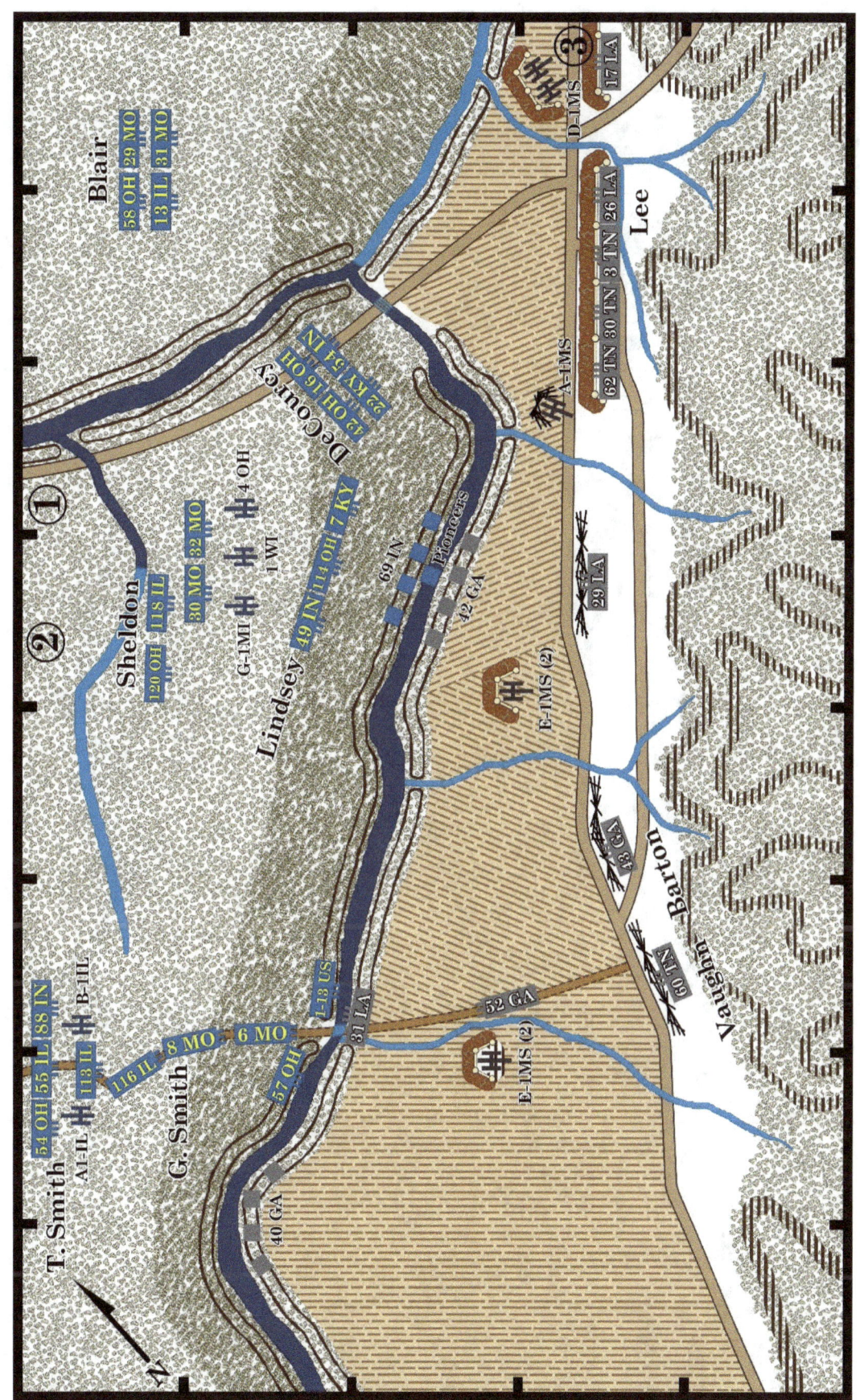

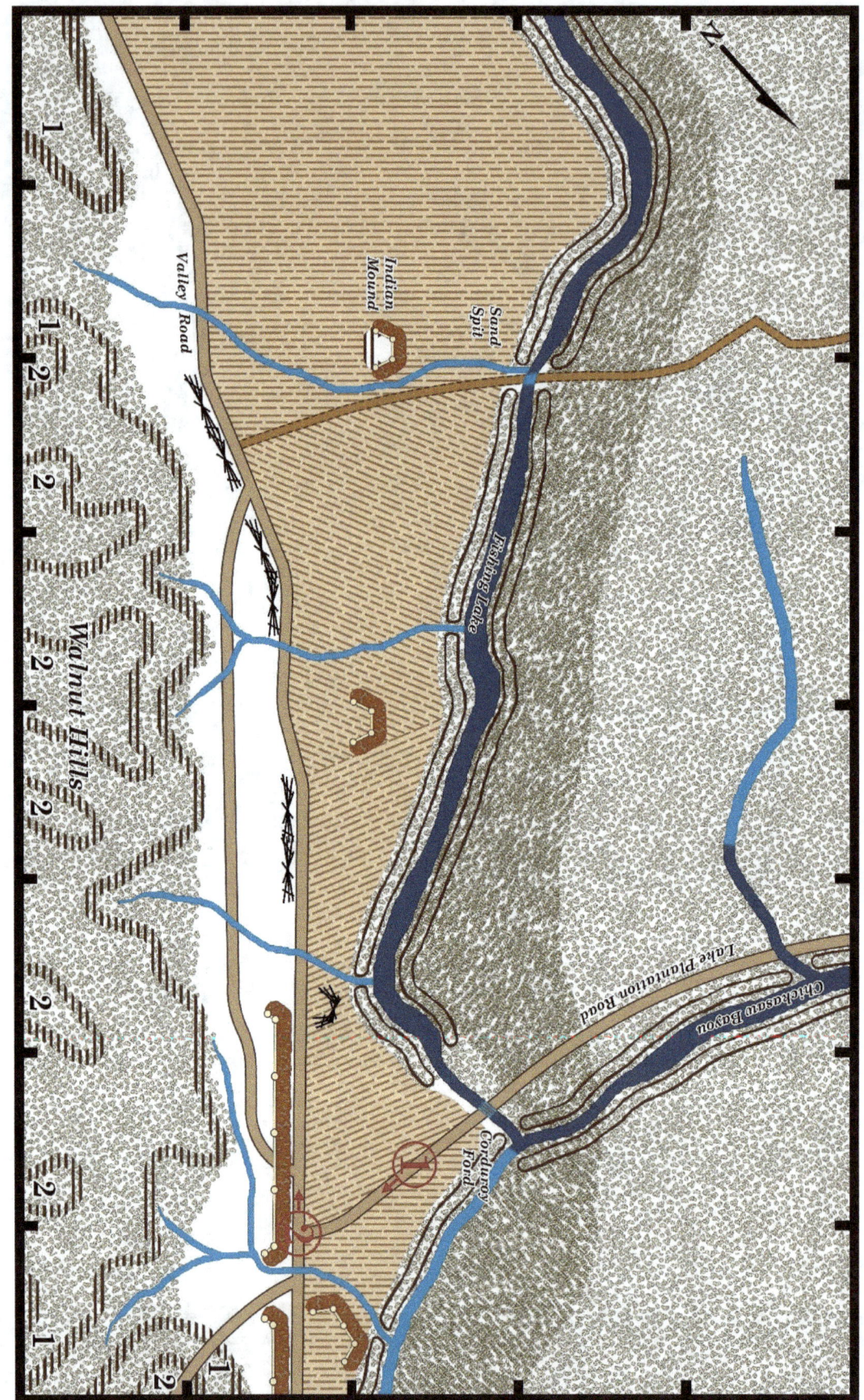

The Battle of Champion Hill: The Crossroads
May 16th, 1863

Background

After Sherman's retreat, Grant spent the remainder of winter and early spring in various attempts to reach Vicksburg. These included an expedition down the Yazoo River to outflank the Walnut Hills, and digging a canal across the hairpin turn of the Mississippi across from Vicksburg. All attempts ended in failure. By April Grant had come to a conclusion: the only way to approach the city was from the south.

By mid-April Grant had his plan in motion. He had a road finished from the supply base at Milliken's Bend north of Vicksburg to the village of Hard Times below the city. On April 16th and 22nd, Admiral David D. Porter floated gunboats and transports down the river past the batteries at Vicksburg, taking only minimal losses. Grant's army marched down the west bank of the river to Hard Times. To disguise the importance of the crossing and confuse the Confederate commander of the Army of Vicksburg, Lieutenant General John C. Pemberton, Grant had Sherman's Fifteenth Corps threaten an assault north of the city, while Colonel Benjamin H. Grierson took off on a cavalry raid down the length of Mississippi. Both ultimately proved successful, especially the cavalry raid, which pulled vital Confederate cavalry from the river and denied Pemberton crucial and timely intelligence of Grant's movements.

On April 30th the army began crossing at Bruinsburg. The next day, May 1st, saw the first battle on the eastern shore at Grand Gulf where General McClernand, now in command of the Thirteenth Corps, defeated a Confederate force sent to block them. From there Grant steadily moved east in a series of starts and stops as he reached one creek and water obstacle after another, as well as waiting for supplies to catch up. Fortunately, Pemberton was slow to react. On May 12th Major General James B. McPherson and his Seventeenth Corps defeated a Confederate force at Raymond. From there Grant

Brigadier General John A. Logan

had a change of plans. He decided on a much wider swing east than originally planned, and moved his army towards the capital of the state at Jackson. Instead of moving to intercept, Pemberton kept his army closer to Vicksburg. Grant captured the capital on May 14th, burned much of it, and destroyed the railroads leading from the city. He then turned west towards Vicksburg.

Pemberton continued to react slowly. Instead of attacking east to help save Jackson, as well as link up with reinforcement arriving under department commander General Joseph E. Johnston, Pemberton instead decided to attack south and intercept Grant's supply trains. Repeated orders from Johnston convinced Pemberton to reverse course and move north, but it was too late. Early on May 16th Grant's arriving army threatened Pemberton's own supply wagons, which moved rapidly west back towards Vicksburg. The Confederates scrambled to establish a defensive line. They found good ground on Champion Hill, a high elevation near the crossroads of the Jackson, Middle, and Ratliff Roads. Unfortunately, it was a race against time. Major General Carter L. Stevenson's large division deployed facing north and east at right angles. One of McClernand's divisions faced them on the Middle Road, but he had orders from Grant not to attack and bring on an engagement

General Logan's view of the battlefield. His division advanced from this position south towards the Confederates on the hill in the background.

until the rest of the army arrived. McPherson arrived and attacked from the north, with Brigadier General John A. Logan outflanking Stevenson's line, and Brigadier General Alvin P. Hovey driving them from the heights.

Just then Brigadier General John S. Bowen's crack division arrived and launched a devastating counterattack, pushing McPherson back and threatening to undo the day's success. McClernand along the Middle Road watched and did nothing, as the messengers from Grant to attack did not arrive. The arrival of another of McPherson's divisions stemmed the grey tide, and forced Bowen to retreat. Pemberton called on his last division, commanded by Major General William W. Loring, to hurry north to maintain the initiative. However, Loring, guarding the road from Raymond, refused to budge citing the gathering Union brigades confronting him. Finally he relented, and sent two brigades north. By the time they arrived, it was too late. McClernand released his divisions along the Middle Road, and Pemberton's men were caught in a vice. Now heavily outnumbered, the Confederate commander ordered a retreat west towards Vicksburg and its strong defenses. Pemberton's only real chance to stop Grant slipped from his grasp: too little in men, too late in the campaign.

Game Overview

Champion Hill is a very large scenario, involving parts of two corps on the Union side. Yet it is popular with wargamers. It is best played over multiple sessions, or a large setting such as a convention.

The board is a bit larger at 5' x 8'. The game begins at 11:00 a.m. and ends when the Confederates are driven from the board, or the Union can no longer attack.

Terrain

The map is dominated by Champion Hill and the ridges along which run the main roads of the region. The first level of hills along the ridges can be gradual and ½ inches in height. They are broken terrain to cross. The main summit of Champion Hill is much steeper. It should be 1 inch in height, and is rough terrain. The woods are thick and should be broken terrain. They are light woods for visibility. The summit is a bit of a conundrum. Grant mentioned that the top of the hill was bare, but Confederate accounts all

Brigadier General John S. Bowen

describe the woods as thick, and an artillery battery stationed at top said, "while, in front, towards the enemy, it was only by peering through the little open spaces that we could locate the enemy." As an alternative, the summit can be bald and devoid of most trees, but it was likely more thickly wooded as indicated on the map.

The fences deduct an inch from visibility. The cornfield does not affect the game. Its only May, and the stalks would just be sprouting, or ankle to knee high at best. The streams deduct an inch from movement, which in the broken woods will slow units down even more.

Deployment

The game begins with the Confederates deployed in a line facing north, then south, with the summit of Champion Hill at the apex. For the Union, Hovey and Logan's divisions may move immediately. Osterhaus' division may not move and must remain in place until released. They may fire at any enemy unit that enters their primary fire zone, but may not charge. They are released and may move freely if charged, or if an enemy unit enters an area that would allow them to deliver partial or full flanking fire upon them. They should not sit there and allow themselves to be destroyed. Otherwise, they are released on Turn [23/16/12]. Lawler's brigade and Battery A, 2nd Illinois arrive next to them at **3** on the same turn.

Stevenson's brigade from Logan's division marches onto the board at **1** on Turn [5/4/3]. Hovey's artillery battalion, minus Battery A, 2nd Illinois with Lawler, enters at **2** in Turn [5/4/3] as well. They can be on the road, or overland on either side of it. Crocker's division enters on the Jackson Road at **2** on Turn [14/10/8] in the following order: Sanborn, Boomer, Holmes, and the 6th Wisconsin Battery. General McPherson may enter the board at any time after Turn [2/2/2], or remain off the map.

On the Confederate side, General Cumming is with the three regiments at the Champion Hill summit. General Stevenson begins the game with him. General Pemberton is at the Roberts house. All rebel units are free to move at any time. General Bowen's division arrives along the Ratliff Road at **4** on Turn [7/5/4], with Cockrell in the lead followed by Green, then the four batteries of the division. General Loring and his division finally arrive at **4** as well on Turn [19/13/10]. Buford's Brigade is in the lead, followed by Featherston. The batteries travel with their brigades.

Victory Conditions

The game ends when either the Confederates are forced from the board, or the Union can no longer advance. If there is no clear winner, add up the Victory Points for enemy units removed. The side with the most Victory Points wins.

Order of Battle

Army of the Tennessee

Thirteenth Army Corps

Ninth Division
BG Peter J. Osterhaus [+2]

1st Brigade	ES	20	30	40	50	100	Status	Arm.
BG Theophilus T. Garrard [+1]	1,162	58	39	29	23	12		
118th Illinois	292	15	10	7	6	3	3	R
49th, 69th Indiana	506	25	17	13	10	5	3	R
7th Kentucky	364	18	12	9	7	4	3	R

2nd Brigade	ES	20	30	40	50	100	Status	Arm.
Col. Daniel W. Lindsey [+1]	1,224	61	41	31	24	12		
16th Ohio, 22nd Kentucky	469	23	16	12	9	5	3	R
42nd Ohio	438	22	15	11	9	4	3	R
114th Ohio	317	16	11	8	6	3	3	R

Twelfth Division
BG Alvin P. Hovey [+2]

1st Brigade	ES	20	30	40	50	100	Status	Arm.
BG George F. McGinnis [+1]	2,371	119	79	59	47	24		
11th Indiana	473	24	16	12	9	5	3	R
24th Indiana	476	24	16	12	10	5	3	R
34th Indiana	510	26	17	13	10	5	3	R
46th Indiana	365	18	12	9	7	4	3	R
29th Wisconsin	547	27	18	14	11	5	3	R

2nd Brigade	ES	20	30	40	50	100	Status	Arm.
Col. James R. Slack [+1]	1,809	90	60	45	36	18		
47th Indiana	441	22	15	11	9	4	3	R
24th Iowa	484	24	16	12	10	5	3	R
28th Iowa	507	25	17	13	10	5	3	R
56th Ohio	377	19	13	9	8	4	3	R

The vital crossroads looking southwest. The road the right is the Jackson Road, leading to Vicksburg. The road to the left, or south, is the Ratliff Road over which Bowen and Loring arrived, marching toward this view point.

Artillery Battalion	ES	Status	Armament
Battery A, 1st Missouri		3	**4x** 6 lb. SB, **2x** 12 lb. H
Battery A, 2nd Illinois		3	**1x** 6 lb. SB, **1x** 10 lb. P, **2x** 14 lbs. JR
2nd Ohio Battery		3	**4x** 6 lb. JR, **2x** 12 lb. H
16th Ohio Battery	111	3	**4x** 6 lb. JR, **2x** 6 lb. SB

Fourteenth Division

2nd Brigade	ES	20	30	40	50	100	Status	Arm.
BG Michael K. Lawler [+1]	1,885	94	63	47	38	19		
21st Iowa	494	25	16	12	10	5	3	R
22nd Iowa	511	26	17	13	10	5	3	R
23rd Iowa	412	21	14	10	8	4	3	R
11th Wisconsin	468	23	16	12	9	5	3	M

Seventeenth Army Corps
MG James B. McPherson [+2]

Third Division
BG John A. Logan [+2]

1st Brigade	ES	20	30	40	50	100	Status	Arm.
BG John E. Smith [+1]	1,626	81	54	41	33	16		
20th, 45th Illinois	476	24	16	12	10	5	3	R
31st Illinois	357	18	12	9	7	4	3	R
124th Illinois	433	22	14	11	9	4	3	R
23rd Indiana	360	18	12	9	7	4	3	R

2nd Brigade	ES	20	30	40	50	100	Status	Arm.
BG Mortimer D. Leggett [+1]	1,486	74	50	37	30	15		
30th Illinois	364	18	12	9	7	4	3	R
20th Ohio	432	22	14	11	9	4	3	R
68th Ohio	360	18	12	9	7	4	3	R
78th Ohio	330	16	11	8	7	3	3	R

3rd Brigade	ES	20	30	40	50	100	Status	Arm.
BG John D. Stevenson [+1]	1,145	57	38	29	23	11		
8th Illinois	280	14	9	7	6	3	3	R
81st Illinois	394	20	13	10	8	4	3	R
32nd Ohio	472	24	16	12	9	5	3	R

Artillery Battalion	ES	Status	Armament
Maj. Charles J. Stolbrand [+1]			
Battery D, 1st Illinois		3	**4x** 24 lb. H
8th Michigan Battery		3	**4x** 6 lb. JR, **2x** 12 lb. H

Seventh Division
BG Marcellus M. Crocker [+1]

1st Brigade	ES	20	30	40	50	100	Status	Arm.
Col. John B. Sanborn [+1]	1,457	73	49	36	29	15		
48th Indiana	323	16	11	8	6	3	3	R
59th Indiana	485	24	16	12	10	5	3	R
4th Minnesota	354	18	12	9	7	4	3	R
18th Wisconsin	295	15	10	7	6	3	3	R

2nd Brigade	ES	20	30	40	50	100	Status	Arm.
Col. Samuel A. Holmes [+1]	1,071	54	36	27	21	11		
17th Iowa	323	16	11	8	6	3	3	R
10th, 24th Missouri	292	15	10	7	6	3	3	R
80th Ohio	456	23	15	11	9	5	3	R

3rd Brigade	ES	20	30	40	50	100	Status	Arm.
Col. George B. Boomer [+1]	1,459	73	49	36	29	15		
93rd Illinois	435	22	15	11	9	4	2	R
5th Iowa	334	17	11	8	7	3	3	R
10th Iowa	383	19	13	10	8	4	3	R
26th Missouri	307	15	10	8	6	3	3	R

Artillery Battalion	ES	Status	Armament
Cpt. Frank C. Sands [+1]			
6th Wisconsin Battery		3	**2x** 6 lb. JR, **2x** 6 lb. SB, **2x** 12 lb. H

Army of Vicksburg
LG John C. Pemberton [+2]

Stevenson's Division
MG Carter L. Stevenson [+2]

First Brigade	ES	20	30	40	50	100	Status	Arm.
BG Seth M. Barton [+1]	1,400	70	47	35	28	14		
40th Georgia	385	19	13	10	8	4	3	R
41st Georgia	412	21	14	10	8	4	3	R
43rd Georgia	287	14	10	7	6	3	3	R
52nd Georgia	316	16	11	8	6	3	3	R

	ES	Status	Armament
Van Den Corput's Georgia Battery		3	**4x** 10 lb. P

Second Brigade	ES	20	30	40	50	100	Status	Arm.
BG Stephen D. Lee [+1]	1,890	95	63	47	38	19		
20th Alabama	421	21	14	11	8	4	3	M
23rd Alabama	300	15	10	8	6	3	3	R
30th Alabama	359	18	12	9	7	4	3	R
31st Alabama	442	22	15	11	9	4	3	R
46th Alabama	368	18	12	9	7	4	3	R

	ES	Status	Armament
Waddell's Alabama Battery		2	**6x** 12 lb. N

Third Brigade	ES	20	30	40	50	100	Status	Arm.
BG Alfred Cummings [+1]	2,483	124	83	62	50	25		
34th Georgia	431	22	14	11	9	4	2	R
36th Georgia	526	26	18	13	11	5	2	M
39th Georgia	462	23	15	12	9	5	2	M
56th Georgia	518	26	17	13	10	5	3	R
57th Georgia	546	27	18	14	11	5	2	R

Artillery Battalion	ES	Status	Armament
Maj. Joseph W. Anderson [+1]			
Botetourt Virginia Battery		3	**1x** 6 lb. SB, **1x** 12 lb. H
Co. A, 1st Mississippi Artillery		3	**2x** 12 lb. N

Loring's Division

MG William W. Loring [+2]

Second Brigade	ES	20	30	40	50	100	Status	Arm.
BG Abraham Buford [+1]	3,005	150	100	75	60	30		
27th Alabama	376	19	13	9	8	4	3	R
35th Alabama	316	16	11	8	6	3	3	R
54th Alabama	498	25	17	12	10	5	2	M
55th Alabama	477	24	16	12	10	5	2	R
9th Arkansas	321	16	11	8	6	3	3	R
3rd Kentucky	335	17	11	8	7	3	3	M
7th Kentucky	338	17	11	8	7	3	3	R
12th Louisiana	344	17	11	9	7	3	3	R

	ES	Status	Armament
Co. A, Pointe Coupee Artillery		3	**2x** 6 lb. R*, **2x** 12 lb. H
Co. C, Pointe Coupee Artillery		3	**4x** 6 lb. SB

*Treat as 6 lb. James Rifles

The Crossroads looking east. To the left of the road would have been the cornfield, across from which Osterhaus waited. Bowen charged from right to left, driving the Union back over Champion Hill to the north.

Third Brigade	ES	20	30	40	50	100	Status	Arm.
BG Winfield S. Featherston [+1]	2,002	100	67	50	40	20		
3rd Mississippi	519	26	17	13	10	5	2	R
22nd Mississippi	422	21	14	11	8	4	3	M
31st Mississippi	431	22	14	11	9	4	3	R
33rd Mississippi	398	20	13	10	8	4	3	R
1st Mississippi Sharpshooter Bn.	232	12	8	6	5	2	3	R

	ES	Status	Armament		
Co. D, 1st Mississippi Artillery		3	**2x** 6 lb. SB, **2x** 12 lb. H		

Bowen's Division
MG John S. Bowen [+2]

First Brigade	ES	20	30	40	50	100	Status	Arm.
Col. Francis M. Cockrell [+1]	2,204	110	73	55	44	22		
1st & 4th Missouri	536	27	18	13	11	5	4	R
2nd Missouri	425	21	14	11	9	4	4	M
3rd Missouri	386	19	13	10	8	4	4	R
5th Missouri	462	23	15	12	9	5	4	R
6th Missouri	395	20	13	10	8	4	4	R

	ES	Status	Armament
Wade's Missouri Battery		3	**6x** 12 lb. N
Landis' Missouri Battery		3	**2x** 12 lb. N
Guibor's Missouri Battery		3	**2x** 6 lb. SB, **2x** 12 lb. H

Second Brigade	ES	20	30	40	50	100	Status	Arm.
BG Martin E. Green [+1]	2,293	115	76	57	46	23		
15th, 19th Arkansas	577	29	19	14	12	6	4	R
20th, 21st Arkansas	581	29	19	15	12	6	3	M
12th Arkansas Sharpshooter Bn.	212	11	7	5	4	2	3	R
1st Arkansas Cavalry Bn.*	378	19	13	9	8	4	3	R
1st, 3rd Missouri Cavalry*	545	27	18	14	11	5	4	R

	ES	Status	Armament
Lowe's Missouri Battery		3	**2x** 6 lb. SB, **2x** 12 lb. H

*Dismounted for the entire game.

Optional Rules

To help simulate the uncertainty of Osterhaus' advance you can vary their release time. Starting at the beginning of Turn [19/13/10] roll one die. If it is in the upper 50%, then Osterhaus is free to move that turn. If not, repeat until it is released. If it is not released by the roll of the die, then they are automatically released on Turn [29/20/15]. Lawler and his battery enter on the same turn Osterhaus is released. Yes, there is the potential they are released early, but also that they are delayed.

Author's Notes

Champion Hill is the major fight of the Vicksburg Campaign, and is a favorite of wargamers. It will be a hard fight for the Confederates, but good use of Bowen's Division can help turn the tide, much as it did in the historic battle. The trick will be to make it stick.

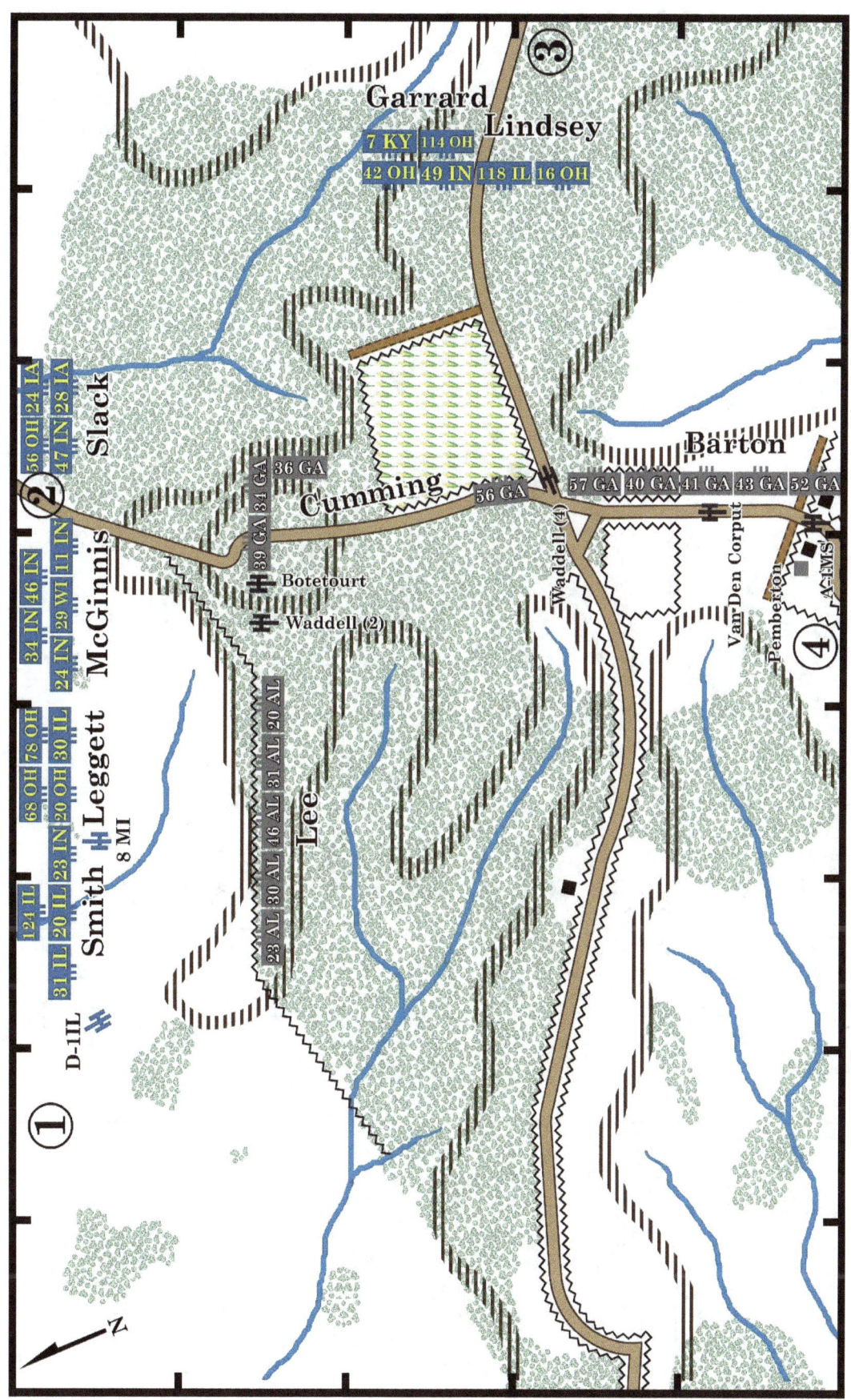

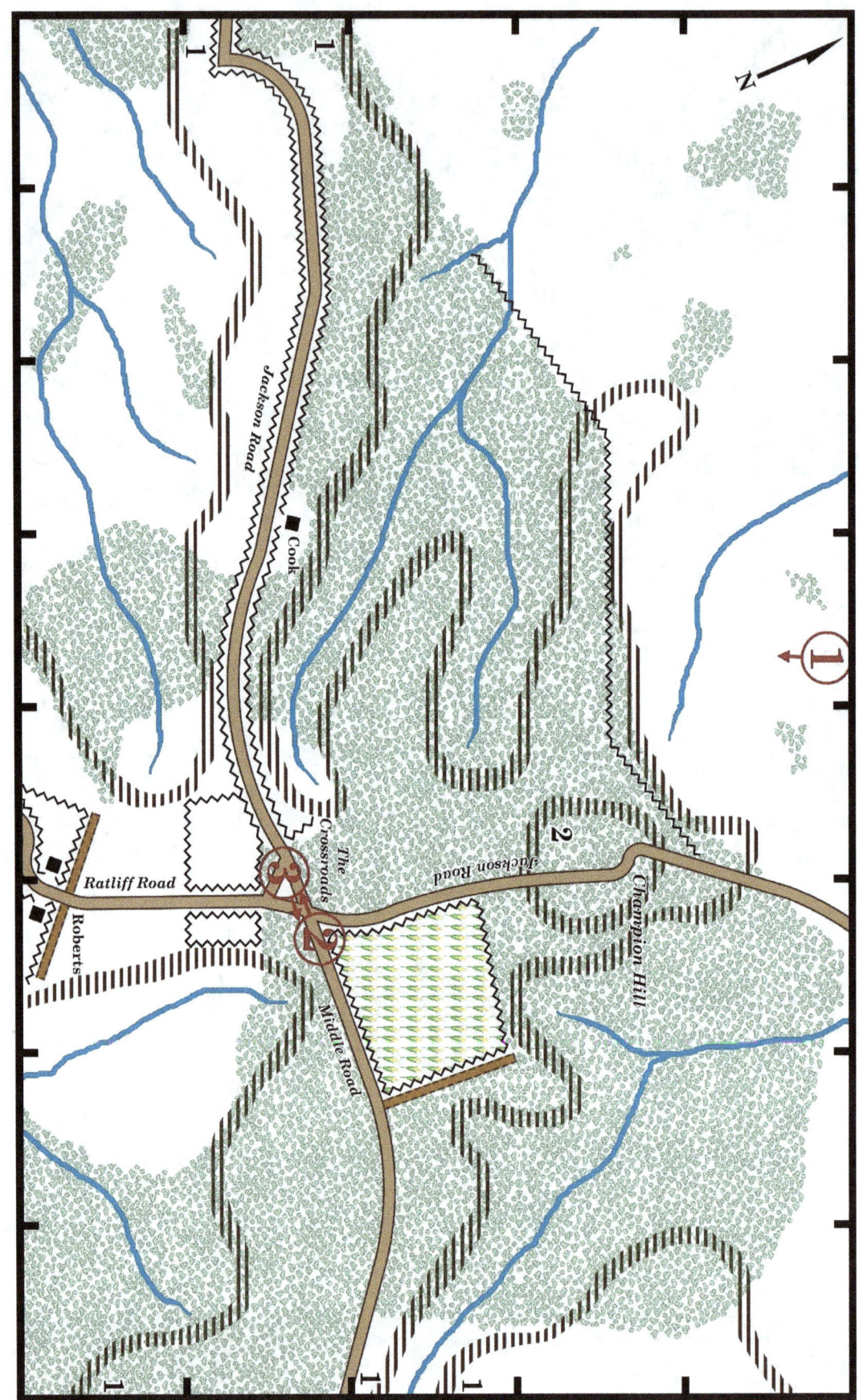

The Battle of Champion Hill: The Coker House

May 16th, 1863

Background

Even before the fighting raged at Champion Hill and The Crossroads to the north, Major General William W. Loring was holding back the advancing Union army along the Raymond Road to the south. Two divisions of General McClernand's Thirteenth Corps had taken the direct road from Raymond to Vicksburg, and Loring was in place to stop them. Brigadier General Andrew J. Smith with his division was in the lead. They drove the Confederate skirmish line past the Sarah Ellison plantation. There, Loring fell back to a low ridge, atop which stood the H. B. Coker house. Much of the space between the Ellison and Coker farms was open, with the Coker house ridge being wooded. An ideal defensive position. Loring deployed his divisional artillery to cover the Raymond Road, and his infantry in support. A. J. Smith continued to skirmish, but he did not have orders to attack. At least not until ordered along with a general advance.

Events further north demanded attention. First Bowen's Division to Loring's left moved north to reinforce the fight at Champion Hill. Then Pemberton sent orders for Loring to join them. Loring demurred. He explained that he was facing considerable forces along the Raymond Road. Pemberton repeated his orders and demanded he march as quickly as possible. Finally, Loring sent two brigade north, but they arrived too late to help Bowen and his counterattack. Historians can only speculate what would have happened if Loring had responded with alacrity.

That left only Brigadier General Lloyd Tilghman and his brigade to cover the Raymond Road. He fell back to a ridge further west, and A. J. Smith advanced with both of his brigades and another in support. Tilghman fell dead during the following artillery duel. From there the brigade fell back and joined Loring, likewise in retreat from the battle at Champion Hill.

Brigadier General Andrew J. Smith

What if Loring's delay had been justified and Smith had been more aggressive? His two brigades would not have arrived at The Crossroads at all, and Bowen and Stevenson would have been smashed by McClernand's delayed attack from the east.

Game Overview

This scenario is a large division sized "what if." The skirmishing around the Coker house was real enough, but what if A. J. Smith had attacked with vigor? Can Loring keep his division together, or can a reinforced Smith punch through and win the southern flank?

The gaming table is 4' x 6'. The game begins at noon and ends when neither side can advance.

Terrain

Most of the high ground on the map is the ridge along the Ratliff Road. This is a gentle elevation. It should only be ½ inch high and gentle or beveled where possible. It only deducts an inch from movement going uphill. The woods are open woods, also only deducting an inch from movement, and are light woods for visibility. Similarly creeks and fences only take an inch to cross. The creeks can be used as cover if a regiment stations itself within its banks.

The Coker House.

Deployment

Deploy the Union and Confederate regiments on the board where shown. Commanders have the discretion to place the individual regiments in their brigade formations where they wish. Loring and Smith begin the game next to any of their units.

The Confederate get 1 Victory Point for any regiment or battery that leaves the board at **2** to go help Pemberton. It can be single regiments, a brigade, or none at all. It's up to the Confederate players. However, they must leave on the road. They won't make it in time if they have to travel overland through the fields.

Landram's brigade enters at **1** on Turn [1/1/1]. He can be in any formation, and can directly enter north or south of the Raymond Road, within reason. Likewise, Blair's division enters at **1** as well on Turn [5/4/3]. They can enter on the road in march column, or one brigade on either side of the road in line or double line. The brigade artillery follows immediately afterwards where there is room.

Major General William W. Loring

Victory Conditions

The game ends when either side is forced from the board. Count up the Victory Points for units lost or commanders killed/removed, as well as Confederate unit sent north to help at Champion Hill. The side with the most points wins.

Order of Battle

Army of the Tennessee

Thirteenth Army Corps

Tenth Division
BG Andrew J. Smith [+2]

1st Brigade	ES	20	30	40	50	100	Status	Arm.
BG Stephen G. Burbridge [+1]	1,289	64	43	32	26	13		
16th Indiana	274	14	9	7	5	3	3	R
67th Indiana	298	15	10	7	6	3	3	R
83rd Ohio	347	17	12	9	7	3	3	R
23rd Wisconsin	370	18	12	9	7	4	3	R

2nd Brigade	ES	20	30	40	50	100	Status	Arm.
Col. William J. Landram [+1]	2,241	112	75	56	45	22		
77th Illinois	411	21	14	10	8	4	3	R
97th Illinois	357	18	12	9	7	4	3	R
108th Illinois	385	19	13	10	8	4	3	R
130th Illinois	371	19	12	9	7	4	3	R
19th Kentucky	458	23	15	11	9	5	3	R
48th Ohio	259	13	9	6	5	3	3	R

Artillery Battalion	ES	Status	Armament
Chicago Mercantile Battery		3	**2x** 6 lb. SB, **2x** 3" R
17th Ohio Battery		3	**6x** 10 lb. P

Fifteenth Army Corps

Second Division
MG Francis Preston Blair, Jr. [+2]

1st Brigade	ES	20	30	40	50	100	Status	Arm.
Col. Giles A. Smith [+1]	1,678	84	56	42	34	17		
113th Illinois	223	11	7	6	4	2	3	R
116th Illinois	333	17	11	8	7	3	3	R
6th Missouri	380	19	13	10	8	4	3	R
8th Missouri	397	20	13	10	8	4	3	R
13th United States, 1st Bn.	345	17	12	9	7	3	3	R

Looking up towards the Confederate artillery position from the base of the hill. The Raymond Road is to the right.

2nd Brigade	ES	20	30	40	50	100	Status	Arm.
Col. Thomas K. Smith [+1]	1,708	85	57	43	34	17		
55th Illinois	409	20	14	10	8	4	3	R
127th Illinois	381	19	13	10	8	4	3	R
83rd Indiana	382	19	13	10	8	4	3	R
54th Ohio	237	12	8	6	5	2	3	R
57th Ohio	299	15	10	7	6	3	3	R

Artillery Battalion	ES	Status	Armament
Battery A, 1st Illinois		3	**4x** 6 lb. SB, **2x** 12 lb. H
Battery B, 1st Illinois		3	**5x** 6 lb. SB, **1x** 12 lb. H

Army of Vicksburg

Loring's Division
MG William W. Loring [+2]

First Brigade	ES	20	30	40	50	100	Status	Arm.
BG Lloyd Tilghman [+1]	1,516	76	51	38	30	15		
6th Mississippi	296	15	10	7	6	3	3	R
15th Mississippi	385	19	13	10	8	4	3	R
23rd Mississippi	322	16	11	8	6	3	3	M
26th Mississippi	308	15	10	8	6	3	3	R
1st Confederate Bn.	205	10	7	5	4	2	2	R

	ES	Status	Armament
Culbertson's Mississippi Battery		3	**2x** 6 lb. SB, **2x** 12 lb. H
Co. G, 1st Mississippi Artillery		3	**4x** 6 lb. SB, **2x** 12 lb. H

Second Brigade	ES	20	30	40	50	100	Status	Arm.
BG Abraham Buford [+1]	3,005	150	100	75	60	30		
27th Alabama	376	19	13	9	8	4	3	R
35th Alabama	316	16	11	8	6	3	3	R
54th Alabama	498	25	17	12	10	5	2	M
55th Alabama	477	24	16	12	10	5	2	R
9th Arkansas	321	16	11	8	6	3	3	R
3rd Kentucky	335	17	11	8	7	3	3	M
7th Kentucky	338	17	11	8	7	3	3	R
12th Louisiana	344	17	11	9	7	3	3	R

	ES	Status	Armament
Co. A, Pointe Coupee Artillery		3	**2x** 6 lb. R*, **2x** 12 lb. H
Co. C, Pointe Coupee Artillery		3	**4x** 6 lb. SB

*Treat as 6 lb. James Rifles

Third Brigade	ES	20	30	40	50	100	Status	Arm.
BG Winfield S. Featherston [+1]	2,002	100	67	50	40	20		
3rd Mississippi	519	26	17	13	10	5	2	R
22nd Mississippi	422	21	14	11	8	4	3	M
31st Mississippi	431	22	14	11	9	4	3	R
33rd Mississippi	398	20	13	10	8	4	3	R
1st Mississippi Sharpshooter Bn.	232	12	8	6	5	2	3	R

	ES	Status	Armament
Co. D, 1st Mississippi Artillery		3	**2x** 6 lb. SB, **2x** 12 lb. H

Optional Rules

There are no optional rules for this scenario.

Author's Notes

The historic skirmish was important, and quite intense. Plus Tilghman was killed nearby. The Coker house is the only surviving structure on the battlefield from 1863. It's a good "what if" with a balanced force size for each side.

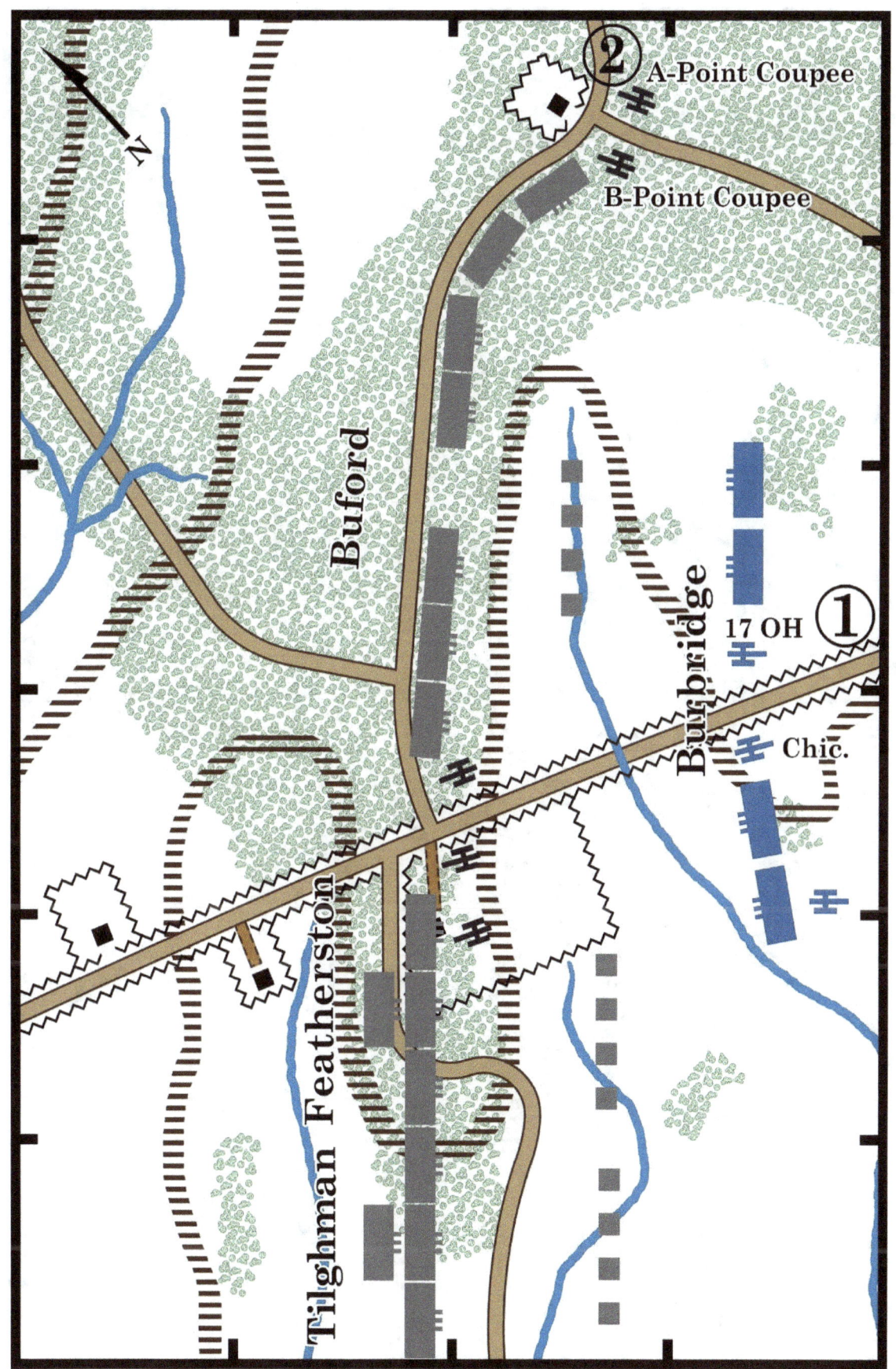

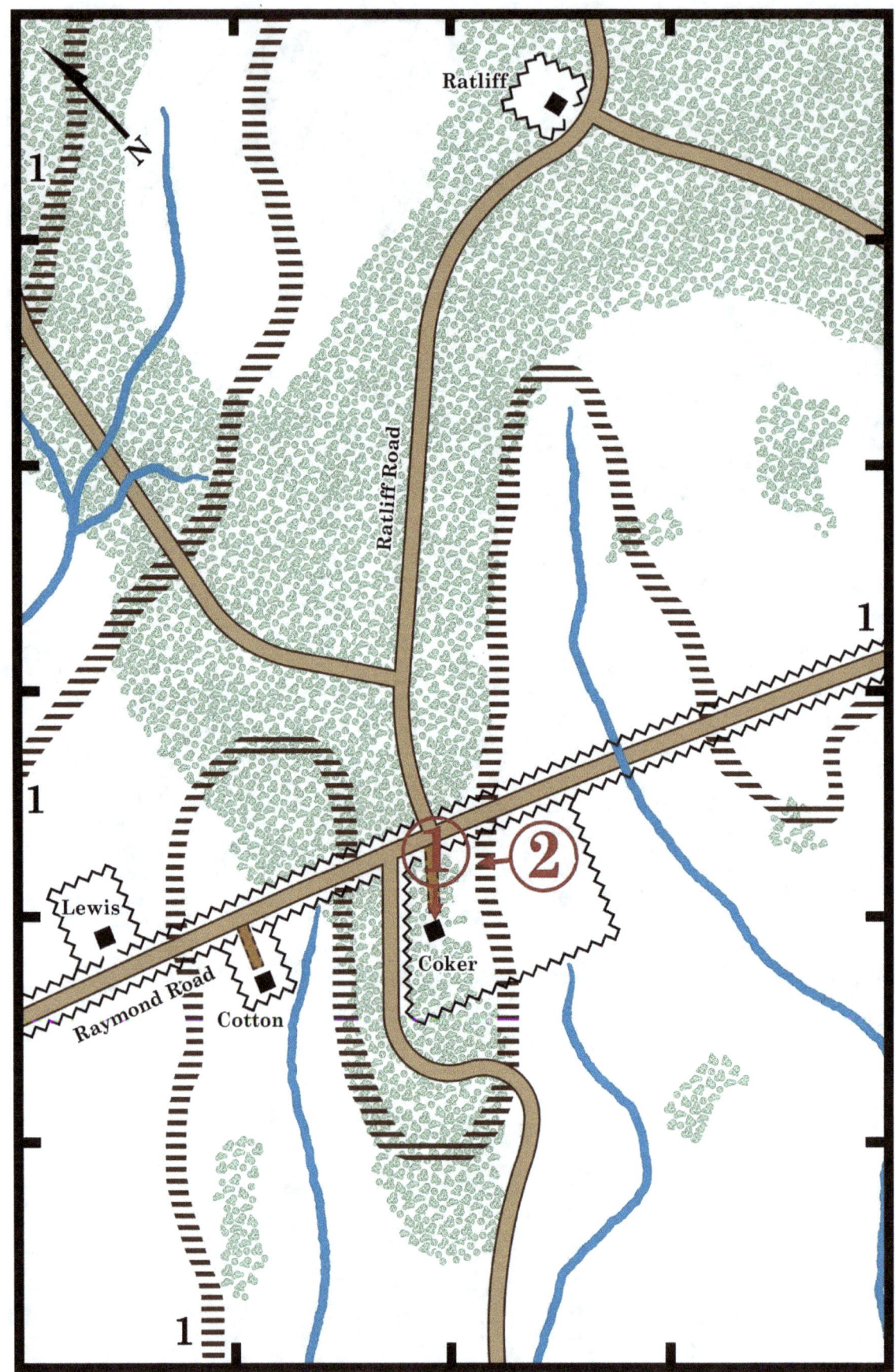

The Battle of Big Black River Bridge
May 17th, 1863

Background

General Pemberton marched his army back towards Vicksburg after his defeat at Champion Hill on May 16th. The last major physical obstacle between the city and Grant's approaching army was the Big Black River. General Loring's division had been cut off from the rest of Pemberton's forces during the chaotic retreat, so the commanding general decided to hold a bridgehead on the east side of the river to allow Loring to catch up and safely cross. Fortunately, there were already defenses built from earlier in the campaign. The men quickly went to work to improve them as they waited for Loring to arrive.

Unfortunately, it was not Loring who approached from the east, but Grant. General McClernand's Thirteenth Corps quickly surrounded the ring of Confederate trenches. The Confederate's main defenses were south of the railroad, where an open field of fire allowed for best use of the available artillery. But to the north, near the bend of the Big Black River, Brigadier General Michael K. Lawler found a covered depression near the river bank that allowed his brigade to seek shelter close to the Confederate line. An aggressive leader, he ordered his brigade to charge the enemy's works without higher orders. The men sprang to their feet and charged diagonally across the enemy's front.

Lawler's charge took them into the midst of Brigadier General John C. Vaughn's East Tennessee brigade. These conscripts showed no taste for fighting, and immediately broke for the rear. This completely broke the Confederate defenses. General Bowen's stalwart division, deployed on each side of Vaughn, had no choice but to retreat once their center was broken. The retreat became a stampede, as the only paths to safety were two bridges over the Big Black River. Over a thousand men were captured, including all of the artillery since their horses had unwisely been moved to the western bank. The tragedy is, Loring was nowhere near the bridge

Brigadier General Michael K. Lawler

and was not marching towards it. He was marching his division away from Vicksburg, and away from the campaign.

It was a humiliating loss for the Confederates, and a morale boosting triumph for the Federals. So far during the campaign, the Union could do no wrong, and encountered no obstacle they could not overcome.

Game Overview

Is a river to your back ever a good defensive position? It worked for Lee at Antietam on the strategic scale, but not so much for Pemberton at Big Black River. This game explores whether the historic outcome was a fluke, or if determined assaults on a strong line can indeed result in defeat for the Union. This is a corps sized game, but still, not too large as the Union divisions are only two brigades each.

The game begins at 11:00 a.m. The game ends when the Confederates are pushed from the board, or the Union can no longer advance.

Terrain

The board is flat with no elevations, so should be easy to set up. The woods are light woods for movement and visibility. The dark bayou in front of the works is broken terrain. The Confederates had filled it with underbrush and abatis as an obstacle. The light bayous only deduct an inch from movement. Both provide a cover bonus for

Modern day view of the north half of the Confederate line. The bayou is long gone. The Confederate works would have been near the line of trees in the middle background. The Union advanced from the right.

any unit taking shelter inside. The Big Black River is impassable.

The fences deduct an inch from movement. The railroad does not affect the game. The swamp is rough terrain. The levee should be small, maybe ½ inch elevation. It has a trail on top running its length. It can serve as hasty works for any unit using it for cover.

The hasty works behind which Lawler is deployed actually represent a depression in the ground which is sheltering the brigade, rather than a complicated lower elevation on an otherwise flat map. Still, treat as hasty works for cover and morale. The Confederate defenses are medium works. There is a small section of hasty works blocking the Jackson Road.

Deployment

Set up the game as shown on the scenario map. All units are on the board. General McClernand can begin next to any Union unit. The Confederates can set up the regiments how they wish within their brigade zones. The historic location of the 1st Missouri Cavalry is indicated on the map, so it should be set up there. The Confederate artillery does not have any limbers. They can be hand pushed only.

Brigadier General John C. Vaughn

Victory Conditions

It's a stand-or-die game. Either the Confederates hold, or they get pushed off the board and lose. There are no Victory Points. The game continues until the Union take so many casualties that they can no longer advance towards the enemy, or they push the rebels off the board.

Order of Battle

Army of the Tennessee

Thirteenth Army Corps
MG John A. McClernand [+2]

Ninth Division
BG Albert L. Lee [+1]

1st Brigade	ES	20	30	40	50	100	Status	Arm.
BG Theophilus T. Garrard [+1]	1,417	71	47	35	28	14		
118th Illinois	287	14	10	7	6	3	3	R
49th, 69th Indiana	467	23	16	12	9	5	3	R
7th Kentucky	341	17	11	9	7	3	3	R
120th Ohio	322	16	11	8	6	3	3	R

2nd Brigade	ES	20	30	40	50	100	Status	Arm.
Col. Daniel W. Lindsey [+1]	1,163	58	39	29	23	12		
16th Ohio, 22nd Kentucky	449	22	15	11	9	4	3	R
42nd Ohio	398	20	13	10	8	4	3	R
114th Ohio	316	16	11	8	6	3	3	R

Artillery Battalion	ES	Status	Armament
Cpt. Jacob T. Foster [+1]			
7th Michigan Battery		3	6x 3" R
1st Wisconsin Battery		3	3x 20 lb. P

Tenth Division
BG Andrew J. Smith [+2]

1st Brigade	ES	20	30	40	50	100	Status	Arm.
BG Stephen G. Burbridge [+1]	1,273	64	42	32	25	13		
16th Indiana	270	14	9	7	5	3	3	R
67th Indiana	292	15	10	7	6	3	3	R
83rd Ohio	344	17	11	9	7	3	3	R
23rd Wisconsin	367	18	12	9	7	4	3	R

The area behind the Confederate works. The Confederate line was in the distance. They had to retreat across this open area to the crossings behind the camera.

2nd Brigade Col. William J. Landram [+1]	ES	20	30	40	50	100	Status	Arm.
	1,850	93	62	46	37	19		
77th Illinois	410	21	14	10	8	4	3	R
97th Illinois	352	18	12	9	7	4	3	R
130th Illinois	371	19	12	9	7	4	3	R
19th Kentucky	458	23	15	11	9	5	3	R
48th Ohio	259	13	9	6	5	3	3	R

Artillery Battalion	ES	Status	Armament
Chicago Mercantile Battery		3	**2x** 6 lb. SB, **2x** 3" R
17th Ohio Battery		3	**6x** 10 lb. P

Twelfth Division

Artillery Battalion	ES	Status	Armament
Battery A, 2nd Illinois		3	**2x** 6 lb. JR

Fourteenth Division

BG Eugene A. Carr [+2]

1st Brigade BG William P. Benton [+1]	ES	20	30	40	50	100	Status	Arm.
	2,060	103	69	52	41	21		
33rd Illinois	467	23	16	12	9	5	3	R
99th Illinois	461	23	15	12	9	5	3	R
8th Indiana	644	32	21	16	13	6	3	R
18th Indiana	488	24	16	12	10	5	3	R

2nd Brigade	ES	20	30	40	50	100	Status	Arm.
BG Michael K. Lawler [+2]	1,869	93	62	47	37	19		
21st Iowa	490	25	16	12	10	5	3	R
22nd Iowa	505	25	17	13	10	5	3	R
23rd Iowa	409	20	14	10	8	4	3	R
11th Wisconsin	465	23	16	12	9	5	3	M

Artillery Battalion	ES	Status	Armament
1st Indiana Battery		3	**4x** 6 lb. JR

Army of Vicksburg

Smith's Division

Second Brigade	ES	20	30	40	50	100	Status	Arm.
BG John C. Vaughn [+1]	1,500	75	50	38	30	15		
60th Tennessee	477	24	16	12	10	5	1	M
61st Tennessee	551	28	18	14	11	6	1	R
62nd Tennessee	472	24	16	12	9	5	1	R

Artillery Battalion	ES	Status	Armament
Co. A, 1st Mississippi Artillery		3	**4x** 10 lb. P

Bowen's Division
MG John S. Bowen [+2]

First Brigade	ES	20	30	40	50	100	Status	Arm.
Col. Francis M. Cockrell [+1]	1,615	81	54	40	32	16		
1st Missouri	361	18	12	9	7	4	4	R
2nd Missouri	342	17	11	9	7	3	4	M
3rd, 6th Missouri	540	27	18	14	11	5	3	R
5th Missouri	372	19	12	9	7	4	3	R

	ES	Status	Armament
Wade's Missouri Battery		3	**4x** 12 lb. N
Guibor's Missouri Battery		3	**2x** 6 lb. SB, **2x** 12 lb. H

Second Brigade	ES	20	30	40	50	100	Status	Arm.
BG Martin E. Green [+1]	2,025	101	68	51	41	20		
15th, 19th Arkansas	512	26	17	13	10	5	3	R
20th, 21st Arkansas	537	27	18	13	11	5	3	M
1st Arkansas Cav Bn.*, 12th AR SS Bn.	527	26	18	13	11	5	3	R
1st, 3rd Missouri Cavalry*	449	22	15	11	9	4	3	R

	ES	Status	Armament		
Dawson's Missouri Battery		3	**2x** 6 lb. SB, **2x** 12 lb. H		
Lowe's Missouri Battery		3	**2x** 6 lb. SB, **2x** 12 lb. H		

*Dismounted for the entire game.

Optional Rules

There are no optional rules for this game.

Author's Notes

The Big Black River is a tragedy in that Loring was never going to arrive. His feud with, and animosity towards, Pemberton led him to decide to take his isolated division away from the army and escape. On a tactical level, the Confederates should have a decent chance to hold their ground. They have a good position and good works. Will Vaughn's men prove the weak point as it did historically? This is why we play wargames, to play this out and see if we can replicate the historic outcome.

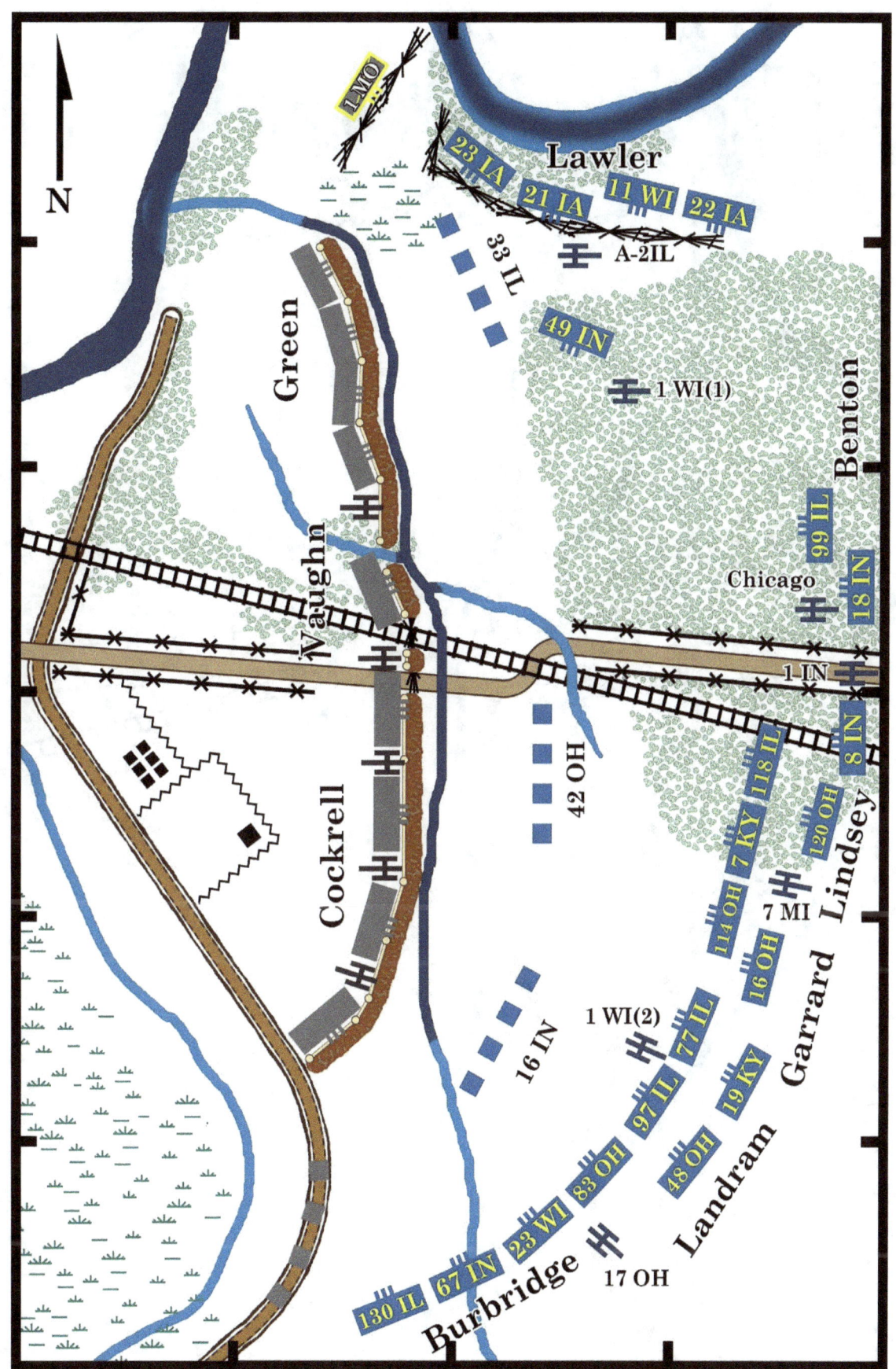

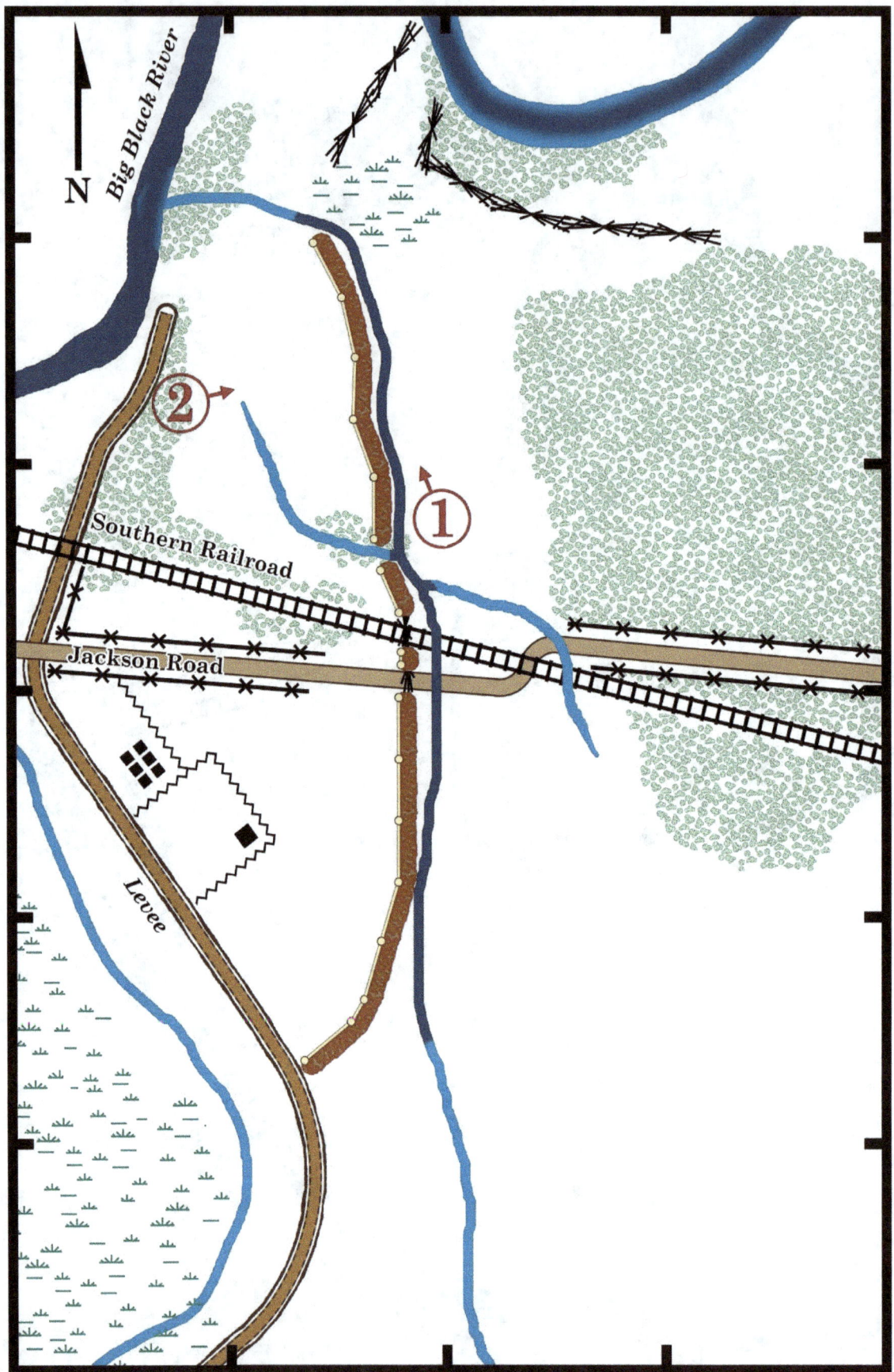

Vicksburg Assault: Sherman May 19th
May 19th, 1863

Background

After the disaster at the Big Black River, Pemberton pulled his Army of Vicksburg back into the city's ring of defenses. They were formidable indeed, and if not complete in some areas, the men went to work with a will to strengthen them before the Yankee horde arrived. The line of trenches and fortifications generally followed ridgelines to the north and east of the city. These were tall, and farming over the last few decades had removed almost all of the vegetation, giving unparalleled open fields of fire to the defenders.

There were six main roads into the city, three of them directly from the east, and upon which Grant approached. The Graveyard Road crossed the Confederate defenses along a narrow ridge where their northern facing line turned sharply south. Further south, across Glass Bayou, was the Jackson Road, the direct route to the capital. South of there was the Baldwin's Ferry Road, which roughly paralleled the Southern Railroad, the city's economic lifeline.

Grant spent May 18th moving his army to and around the city. It was tough going, as the off-road ridges and draws were extremely difficult to maneuver through. The commanding general wanted to capture Vicksburg quickly. Surmising that the stunning string of defeats the past month must have demoralized the Confederates, Grant determined to assault the rebel defenses while they were still reeling. He set 2:00 p.m. on the 19th as the jump off for a grand assault along the lines.

As the time neared the next day, reality soon hit. Only Sherman along the Graveyard Road was in any position to launch an attack. The signal cannons fired, and Major General Francis Preston Blair, Jr.'s division stepped off with a will. But all the determination and willpower in the world can be stymied by the worst terrain. Guarding the Graveyard Road was a large fortification, or redan, known as the Stockade Redan, manned by troops from Brigadier General Francis A.

Major General Francis P. Blair Jr.

Shoup's Brigade. These men, and the ones manning the fortifications for most of the line, were not the demoralized rebels who had fought at Champion Hill and Big Black River. They were fresh troops yet to see action.

The only approach to the Stockade Redan was the very narrow ridgeline upon which the road lay. At its narrowest just before the Stockade Redan it is 15 yards wide at best. As a result, Blair's brigades had to move through the deep, steep ravines on either side. It was slow going, and the Confederates had thrown down whatever brush and trees they had to form obstacles and abatis.

The terrain defeated Blair just as much as the rebels. Three brigades advanced towards the Stockade Redan and it surrounding fortifications, but the Union men could make no headway against the steep slopes, obstacles, and Confederate fire. Even when they reached the redan and rebel lines, they found it impossible to scale the deep outer ditches and near vertical walls of the forts. One Illinoisan wrote, "when we got to the fort we could not climb it the fort is 15 feet high and a big ditch on this side 5 feet deep & 7 wide." Soon all involved realized the attack had failed. Those closest to the works had to endure the blistering sunshine for the rest of the day, with nowhere to go. Retreat would have been suicide. Finally darkness fell, and most of the men were able to fall back during the night to safer line.

In truth, of all three corps that were supposed to attack that day, only Blair's division and

Looking from the ramparts of the Stockade Redan down the Graveyard Road towards the Union approach. The narrow ridge forced the Union soldiers of T. Kilby Smith's brigade into the ravines to the left and right.

Brigadier General Thomas E. G. Ransom's supporting brigade made any true assault. It would take better coordination and determination to break through the Vicksburg defenses.

Game Overview

This and the next series of scenarios explore the tactical problem of attacking and capturing prepared works. That is much of the heart of what Vicksburg is all about. The game is a division sized scenario. Other than the set-up time with its works and obstacles, it should be playable in one session.

The game starts at 2:00 p.m. and ends when the Union breach the works and cause the Confederates to fall back, or the Union can no longer advance.

Terrain

The terrain for the map is a series of ridges. The Graveyard Road runs atop one of them, and the rest are cut through by various waterways such as the Mint Springs and Glass Bayous.

While the maps provided look detailed, and can provide a good representation of the ground if done in full, absolutely feel free to simplify the elevations for an easier set-up. For visual ease, the first level elevations are a light tan color, and the second level are the usual dark brown. For a quicker game, it might even be easier to eliminate the first level elevations altogether. The elevations should be a full 1 inch tall, and are rough terrain to cross. The first level elevations in front of the works can provide cover and block line of sight. The second elevations just in front of the works do not. The Confederates should be able to see any attacking unit all the way to the first elevation. The narrow neck of the ridge in front of the Stockade Redan and along the Graveyard Road should be too small for a regiment to cross in line of battle, or even double line, assault column, or disorder, without spilling over the sides and having to use rough terrain movement. A regiment in march column along the road would be unaffected.

The Confederate trenches are heavy works. In front of them is a line of felled trees and obstacles in an abatis. Most rules should have their own

Brigadier General Francis A. Shoup

built in mechanics for negotiating the difficulties in crossing both obstacles. It may seem unrealistic to have open terrain between the two elevation levels, but if you abstract the rough terrain of the slopes themselves, and the combined obstacles of the abatis and heavy works, it should all balance out for a workable wargame. The same goes for the subsequent Vicksburg scenarios.

What woods are on the map are open woods. They only deduct and inch from movement, and are light woods for visibility. The two bayous are different. They are steep and brushy along their banks. They are rough terrain to cross. Yet another terrible obstacle. The Union artillery are behind hasty works.

Deployment

Set up the map as shown. Blair and Sherman begin the game at the crossroads in the rear. Some rules allow troops behind works to spread out with no penalties. If possible, let the Confederate regiments to expand their frontage while in their trenches. Take advantage of this to fill the spaces in the lunettes, and in and around the single cannon (or section, see next). Also, the order of battle lists many single cannon. If the minimum artillery unit is a single section (two cannon) for the rules being played, feel free to use a section instead of a single gun. Cockrell's Brigade, in reserve, can conform to the terrain so that the regiments are not deployed on the slopes themselves, allowing for quicker movement while in reserve.

Victory Conditions

The game continues until the Confederates are forced to withdraw from the map, or the Union can no longer advance, based upon the command and control rules being played.

Order of Battle

Army of the Tennessee

Fifteenth Army Corps
MG William T. Sherman [+2]

Second Division
MG Francis Preston Blair, Jr. [+2]

1st Brigade	ES	20	30	40	50	100	Status	Arm.
Col. Giles A. Smith [+1]	1,678	84	56	42	34	17		
113th Illinois	223	11	7	6	4	2	3	R
116th Illinois	333	17	11	8	7	3	3	R
6th Missouri	380	19	13	10	8	4	3	R
8th Missouri	397	20	13	10	8	4	3	R
13th United States, 1st Bn.	345	17	12	9	7	3	3	R

The Union view of the Graveyard Road, the narrow ridge, and the Stockade Redan in the background.

2nd Brigade	ES	20	30	40	50	100	Status	Arm.
Col. Thomas K. Smith [+1]	1,708	85	57	43	34	17		
55th Illinois	409	20	14	10	8	4	3	R
127th Illinois	381	19	13	10	8	4	3	R
83rd Indiana	382	19	13	10	8	4	3	R
54th Ohio	237	12	8	6	5	2	3	R
57th Ohio	299	15	10	7	6	3	3	R

3rd Brigade	ES	20	30	40	50	100	Status	Arm.
BG Hugh Ewing [+1]	2,033	102	68	51	41	20		
30th Ohio	443	22	15	11	9	4	3	R
37th Ohio	538	27	18	13	11	5	3	R
47th Ohio	452	23	15	11	9	5	2	R
4th West Virginia	600	30	20	15	12	6	2	R

Artillery Battalion	ES	Status	Armament
Battery A, 1st Illinois		3	**5x** 12 lb. N, **1x** 10 lb. P
Battery B, 1st Illinois		3	**4x** 6 lb. SB, **2x** 12 lb. H
Battery H, 1st Illinois		3	**4x** 20 lb. P

Seventeenth Army Corps
Sixth Division

2nd Brigade	ES	20	30	40	50	100	Status	Arm.
BG Thomas E. G. Ransom [+1]	1,947	97	65	49	39	19		
11th Illinois	491	25	16	12	10	5	3	R
72nd Illinois	391	20	13	10	8	4	2	R
95th Illinois	428	21	14	11	9	4	2	R
14th Wisconsin	209	10	7	5	4	2	3	R
17th Wisconsin	428	21	14	11	9	4	3	R

Army of Vicksburg

Smith's Division
MG Martin L. Smith [+2]

Baldwin's Brigade	ES	20	30	40	50	100	Status	Arm.
BG William E. Baldwin [+1]	1,020	51	34	26	20	10		
31st Louisiana	533	27	18	13	11	5	3	M
46th Mississippi	487	24	16	12	10	5	3	R

Shoup's Brigade	ES	20	30	40	50	100	Status	Arm.
BG Francis A. Shoup [+1]	1,093	55	36	27	22	11		
26th Louisiana	512	26	17	13	10	5	3	R
27th Louisiana	581	29	19	15	12	6	2	R

Artillery	ES	Status	Armament
McNally's Arkansas Battery		3	1x 12 lb. H

Forney's Division
MG John H. Forney [+2]

Hébert's Brigade	ES	20	30	40	50	100	Status	Arm.
BG Louis Hébert [+1]	1,849	92	62	46	37	18		
36th Mississippi	302	15	10	8	6	3	3	M
37th Mississippi	421	21	14	11	8	4	3	M
38th Mississippi	387	19	13	10	8	4	3	M
43rd Mississippi	455	23	15	11	9	5	3	M
7th Mississippi Bn.	284	14	9	7	6	3	3	M

Artillery	ES	Status	Armament
Wall's Texas Battery		3	**1x** Whitworth Rifle
Appeal's Arkansas Battery		3	**1x** 12 lb. H

Bowen's Division

First Brigade Col. Francis M. Cockrell [+1]	ES	20	30	40	50	100	Status	Arm.
	1,215	61	40	30	24	12		
1st Missouri	307	15	10	8	6	3	3	R
2nd Missouri	322	16	11	8	6	3	4	M
3rd, 5th Missouri	316	16	11	8	6	3	3	R
6th Missouri	269	13	9	7	5	3	3	R

Optional Rules

Simplifying the elevations as described by removing the first level may help for a quicker game.

Brigadier General Ralph P. Buckland's Third Division brigade was brought forward to support Blair, but once the assault failed he was not committed. One optional rule is to allow Buckland to enter the board. It may just give the Union the extra strength to win. Allow them to enter at 1 on Turn [13/9/7].

Third Division

1st Brigade BG Ralph P. Buckland [+1]	ES	20	30	40	50	100	Status	Arm.
	1,656	83	55	41	33	17		
114th Illinois	531	27	18	13	11	5	2	R
93rd Indiana	412	21	14	10	8	4	3	R
72nd Ohio	375	19	12	9	7	4	3	R
95th Ohio	339	17	11	8	7	3	2	R

Author's Notes

Vicksburg is all about the siege and assaults on the strong fortifications guarding the city. This and the next five scenarios (here and at Port Hudson) explore the tactical problems of trying to attack troops behind strong works. It might not be everyone's favorite wargame to attack works, but it does provide a look into what these men had to endure during the war. These type of grand assaults against prepared, fortified positions should be played at least once to get a feel for what the men went through.

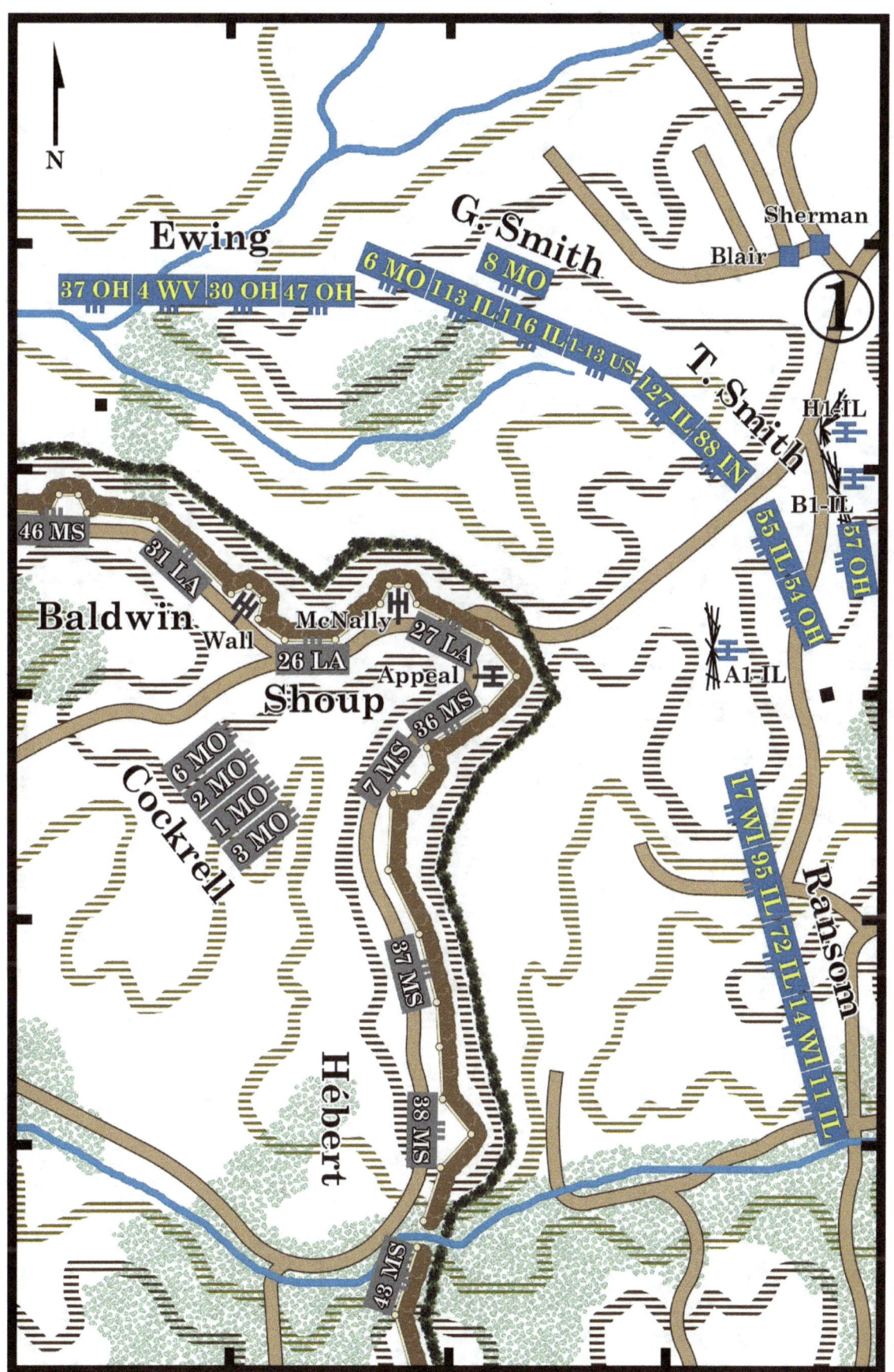

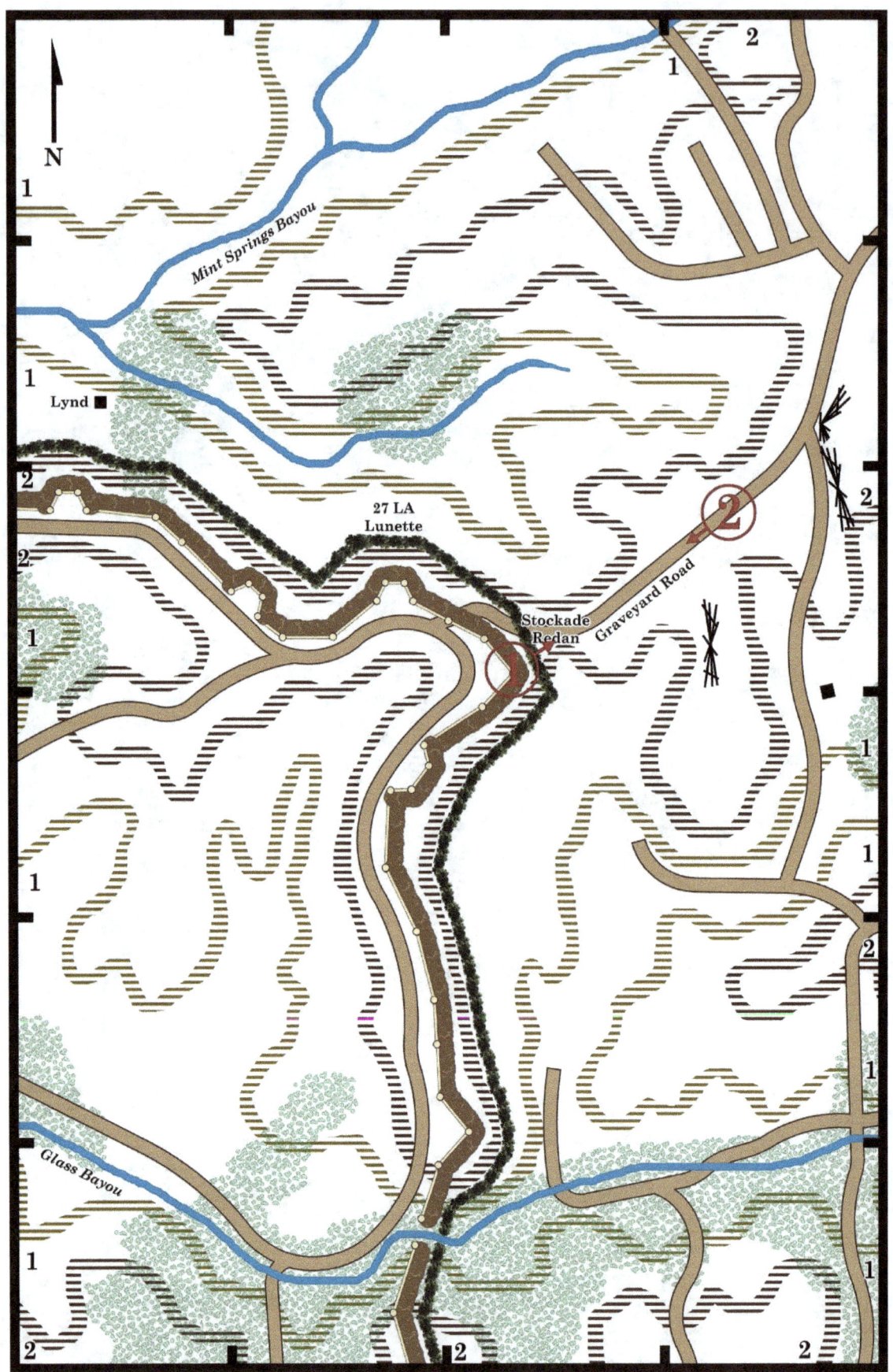

Vicksburg Assault: Sherman May 22nd
May 22nd, 1863

Background

With the failure of the May 19th assaults, Grant took stock of the situation and decided his next move. He still wanted to capture Vicksburg quickly, and thought the Confederates might be on the breaking point. The attacks had failed because he hadn't given his army enough time to deploy and get into position in order to attack all at once. Therefore, Grant decided once again to go for the quick attack and victory. This time all three corps of his army would simultaneously. The attack was set at 10:00 a.m. on the 22nd. Plenty of time for Sherman, McPherson, and McClernand to get their men in position, close up to the works, and be ready to go in one large, blue wave.

Unfortunately, the same conditions in place on the 19th were still there. The majority of the Confederates in the trenches remained fresh. All of them were riding on the high of the May 19th repulse. Any damage from Union artillery was easily repaired at night. In Sherman's front, Brigadier General Francis M. Cockrell's Missouri brigade, in reserve on the 19th, was now in the front lines manning the trenches. The defenses around the Stockade Redan were stronger than three days before.

Sherman decided on a few different tactics. His main hammer would still be General Blair and his division. Instead of deploying in the treacherous ravines, they were to run straight down the road in column and deploy directly in front of the Stockade Redan. Speed would replace formation in the bid to close with the enemy. At the head of the column would run a special unit of volunteers, 50 men from each brigade in the division. This "forlorn hope" would carry bridging material, "boards and poles to cross the ditch," which should help to span the large ditches and make scaling the near vertical walls a little bit easier. Major General Frederick Steele's division would also join the assault, and attack from the north. Brigadier General James M. Tuttle's division would support Blair as needed.

Brigadier General Hugh Ewing

The attack would be proceeded by an artillery bombardment. Things still did not go as planned. The attack started promptly at 10 o'clock. The forlorn hope and the 30th Ohio dashed forward along the road, and were met with a blistering fire at point blank range. Still, they managed to gain the parapet of the Stockade Redan. But that's where the attack fell apart. The following regiment stopped in the middle of the road under fire and went to ground. The remaining regiments jammed up behind them and all refused to move. Finally their commanders got them to deploy into the ravines to the left of the road, eventually linking up with Ransom's brigade to the south. It became a replay of May 19th. With the momentum gone, they made no further progress.

General Steele had difficulty getting into position on time. Brigadier General John M. Thayer's men were in position, but the rest of the division had to struggle through the same steep, up and down terrain to get behind him, leaving only a thin screen to contain the Confederates on the main line to the west up to the Mississippi River. When they did arrive, Blair's attack had already failed.

Matters to the south now took a hand in the battle. Like Sherman, McPherson and McClernand made little headway against the defenders. However, McClernand sent an erroneous report to Grant that he had been successful. He magnified a marginal foothold in one of the larger forts into more of a victory than

The forlorn hope and 30th Ohio's view of the Stockade Redan as they emerged from a slight sunken bend in the road. It is here that the assault fell apart as subsequent regiments refused to move past this point.

it actually was, and asked for more support. Grant had to take his corps commander at his word, and ordered renewed assaults along the lines at 2:00 p.m. Blair, Ransom, and Steele attacked, but the results were the same. They just could not overcome the massive works confronting them. The attacks faltered, and the men again waited for the cover of darkness to withdraw.

Game Overview

Set up the game as shown. This time it's a corps sized attempt to storm the Stockade Redan and surrounding fortifications.

The game starts at 9:00 a.m. and ends when the Union breach the works and cause the Confederates to fall back, or the Union can no longer advance.

Terrain

The terrain for the map is a series of ridges. The Graveyard Road runs atop one of them, and the rest are cut through by various waterways such as the Mint Springs and Glass Bayous. The maps look detailed, and can provide a good representation of the ground, feel free to simplify the elevations for an easier set-up. The first level elevations are a light tan color, and the second level are the usual dark brown. For a quicker game, eliminate the first level elevations altogether. The elevations should be a full 1 inch tall, and are rough terrain to cross. The first level elevations in front of the works can provide cover and block line of sight. The second elevations just in front of the works do not. The Confederates should be able to see any attacking unit all the way to the first elevation. The narrow neck of the ridge in front of the Stockade Redan and along the Graveyard Road should be too small for a regiment to cross in line of battle, or even double line, assault column, or disorder, without spilling over the sides and having to use rough terrain movement. A regiment in march column along the road would be unaffected.

The Confederate trenches are heavy works. In front of them is a line of felled trees and obstacles in an abatis. Most rules should have their own built in mechanics for negotiating the difficulties in crossing both obstacles. It may seem unrealistic to have open terrain between the two elevation levels, but if you abstract the rough

Brigadier General Francis M. Cockrell

terrain of the slopes themselves, and the combined obstacles of the abatis and heavy works, it should all balance out for a workable wargame.

The Union artillery is now dug in behind medium works. Battery E, 1st Illinois is on a slight rise that is impossible to replicate accurately. They have line of sight over above the 2nd Iowa Battery in front of them and can fire over their heads. They can fire at anything two inches and beyond the front of the 2nd Iowa's works without having to roll or otherwise accidently hit the friendly battery. Anything closer and the rules for firing through friendly units apply.

What woods are on the map are open woods. They only deduct an inch from movement. The two bayous are different. They are steep and brushy along their banks. They are rough terrain to cross. Yet another terrible obstacle. The Union artillery are behind hasty works.

The Ann Lynd house is now in ruins. It was burned down during the May 19th assault to deny its use to the Federals.

Deployment

Set up the board as shown. The game begins at 9 a.m. with a Union artillery bombardment of the Confederate works. Thayer and Ransom may not move. At 10 a.m. the attack begins. Thayer and Ransom may attack, although Thayer does know that the rest of his division is on its way. They are just late.

Blair's division enters at **1** in march column. The forlorn hope is in the lead. On the road, they are in march column, and move as such. Off-road, they are always considered in skirmish formation. Any unit touching them, up to a maximum of two regiments (theoretically one on each side) gets a slight additional bonus for attacking, crossing, or charging enemy works. This will vary by game, so no concrete rule is provided here, but don't make the advantage too great. Just better than an un-aided assault.

Ewing follows after the forlorn hope in march column in the following order: 30th Ohio, 37th Ohio, 4th West Virginia, and 47th Ohio. Giles Smith enters next, followed by T. Kilby Smith. Blair begins the game where shown. Colonel Col. Charles R. Wood's brigade arrives and marches onto the board at **2** on Turn [19/13/10]. Instead of waiting until 2 o'clock and the rest of the division, the brigade can attack immediately. However, they are slightly fatigued and worn out from the morning's march through difficult terrain.

If the rules let units behind works to spread out without penalty, use this to allow the Confederate regiments to expand their frontage while in their trenches. Take advantage of this to fill the spaces in the lunettes, and in and around the cannon in the fortifications. The order of battle lists many single cannon. If the minimum artillery unit is a single section (two cannon) for the rules being played, feel free to use a section instead of a single gun. Historically the Whitworth cannon from Waul's Battery burst on May 19th and was replaced by the 3" Ordnance rifle from Company C, 1st Mississippi. The Confederates may move beginning Turn [1/1/1], and redeploy if they wish.

Victory Conditions

The game continues until the Confederates are forced to withdraw from the map, or the Union can no longer advance, based upon the command and control rules being played.

Order of Battle

Army of the Tennessee

Fifteenth Army Corps
MG William T. Sherman [+2]

First Division

2nd Brigade	ES	20	30	40	50	100	Status	Arm.
Col. Charles R. Wood [+1]	2,503	125	83	63	50	25		
25th Iowa	526	26	18	13	11	5	3	R
31st Iowa	397	20	13	10	8	4	2	R
3rd Missouri	334	17	11	8	7	3	3	R
12th Missouri	423	21	14	11	8	4	2	R
17th Missouri	324	16	11	8	6	3	2	R
76th Ohio	499	25	17	12	10	5	3	R

3rd Brigade	ES	20	30	40	50	100	Status	Arm.
BG John M. Thayer [+1]	1,384	69	46	35	28	14		
4th Iowa	375	19	12	9	7	4	3	M
9th Iowa	341	17	11	9	7	3	3	R
26th Iowa	300	15	10	8	6	3	3	R
30th Iowa	368	18	12	9	7	4	3	R

Second Division

MG Francis Preston Blair, Jr. [+2]

1st Brigade	ES	20	30	40	50	100	Status	Arm.
Col. Giles A. Smith [+1]	1,201	60	40	30	24	12		
113th Illinois	216	11	7	5	4	2	3	R
116th Illinois	262	13	9	7	5	3	3	R
6th Missouri	352	18	12	9	7	4	3	R
8th Missouri	371	19	12	9	7	4	3	R

Steele's assault against the Confederate line. They had to charge up this steep slope to reach the Confederates at the top.

2nd Brigade Col. Thomas K. Smith [+1]	ES	20	30	40	50	100	Status	Arm.
	1,553	78	52	39	31	16		
55th Illinois	383	19	13	10	8	4	3	R
127th Illinois	341	17	11	9	7	3	3	R
83rd Indiana	326	16	11	8	7	3	3	R
54th Ohio	222	11	7	6	4	2	3	R
57th Ohio	281	14	9	7	6	3	3	R

3rd Brigade BG Hugh Ewing [+1]	ES	20	30	40	50	100	Status	Arm.
	1,929	96	64	48	39	19		
Forlorn Hope*	150	8	5	4	3	2	4	R
30th Ohio	434	22	14	11	9	4	3	R
37th Ohio	489	24	16	12	10	5	3	R
47th Ohio	393	20	13	10	8	4	3	R
4th West Virginia	463	23	15	12	9	5	3	R

*50 men from each brigade in the division.
Bonus to scaling/combating heavy works to any regiment touching the Forlorn Hope.

Artillery Battalion	ES	Status	Armament
Battery A, 1st Illinois		3	**5x** 12 lb. N, **1x** 10 lb. P
Battery B, 1st Illinois		3	**5x** 6 lb. SB, **1x** 12 lb. H
Battery H, 1st Illinois		3	**2x** 20 lb. P

Third Division

Artillery Battalion	ES	Status	Armament
Battery E, 1st Illinois		3	**4x** 6 lb. JR, **3x** 6 lb. SB
2nd Iowa Battery		3	**2x** 6 lb. SB, **2x** 12 lb. H

Seventeenth Army Corps
Sixth Division

2nd Brigade	ES	20	30	40	50	100	Status	Arm.
BG Thomas E. G. Ransom [+1]	1,823	91	61	46	36	18		
11th Illinois	479	24	16	12	10	5	3	R
72nd Illinois	387	19	13	10	8	4	3	R
95th Illinois	366	18	12	9	7	4	3	R
14th, 17th Wisconsin	591	30	20	15	12	6	3	R

Army of Vicksburg

Smith's Division
MG Martin L. Smith [+2]

Baldwin's Brigade	ES	20	30	40	50	100	Status	Arm.
BG William E. Baldwin [+1]	975	49	33	24	20	10		
31st Louisiana	512	26	17	13	10	5	3	M
46th Mississippi	463	23	15	12	9	5	3	R

Shoup's Brigade	ES	20	30	40	50	100	Status	Arm.
BG Francis A. Shoup [+1]	1,046	52	35	26	21	10		
26th Louisiana	491	25	16	12	10	5	3	R
27th Louisiana	555	28	19	14	11	6	2	R

Artillery	ES	Status	Armament
McNally's Arkansas Battery		3	**1x** 12 lb. H

Looking from the redoubt south of the Stockade Redan toward the Graveyard Road to the north. You can see the steep ravine Blair's division had to deploy into, then march up and attack the Confederates from there.

Forney's Division

Hébert's Brigade	ES	20	30	40	50	100	Status	Arm.
BG Louis Hébert [+1]	1,754	88	58	44	35	18		
36th Mississippi	286	14	10	7	6	3	3	M
37th Mississippi	408	20	14	10	8	4	3	M
38th Mississippi	368	18	12	9	7	4	3	M
43rd Mississippi	433	22	14	11	9	4	3	M
7th Mississippi Bn.	259	13	9	6	5	3	3	M

Artillery	ES	Status	Armament
Company C, 1st Mississippi Artillery		3	**1x** 3" R
Appeal's Arkansas Battery		3	**1x** 12 lb. H

Bowen's Division

First Brigade Col. Francis M. Cockrell [+1]	ES	20	30	40	50	100	Status	Arm.
	1,150	58	38	29	23	12		
1st Missouri	284	14	9	7	6	3	4	R
2nd Missouri	311	16	10	8	6	3	4	M
3rd, 5th Missouri	303	15	10	8	6	3	3	R
6th Missouri	252	13	8	6	5	3	4	R

Optional Rules

This can be played as a sequel of sorts to the May 19th scenario. Play the May 19th game and keep track of the casualties for each regiment. Return 10%, rounded up, to represent lightly wounded and those returning to the regiment after having been separated. Use this for the new regimental strengths. Don't worry too much about deducting for the forlorn hope. Just use the 150 men without reducing the brigades any further.

Alternately, you can dispense with the forlorn hope altogether.

Author's Notes

On one hand, the Union have more brigades available on the 22nd. However, the Confederates also have more regiments in the works. However, because of that, they no longer have a reserve. It's going to be another tough fight for the Union.

I decided against drawing out the game into the renewed 2 o'clock attack. It would take too much messing with the timeline, or make an overly long game. The same thinking went into the next McPherson and McClernand scenarios. The concentration is on how they began their 10 o'clock attacks, and handled the battle from there.

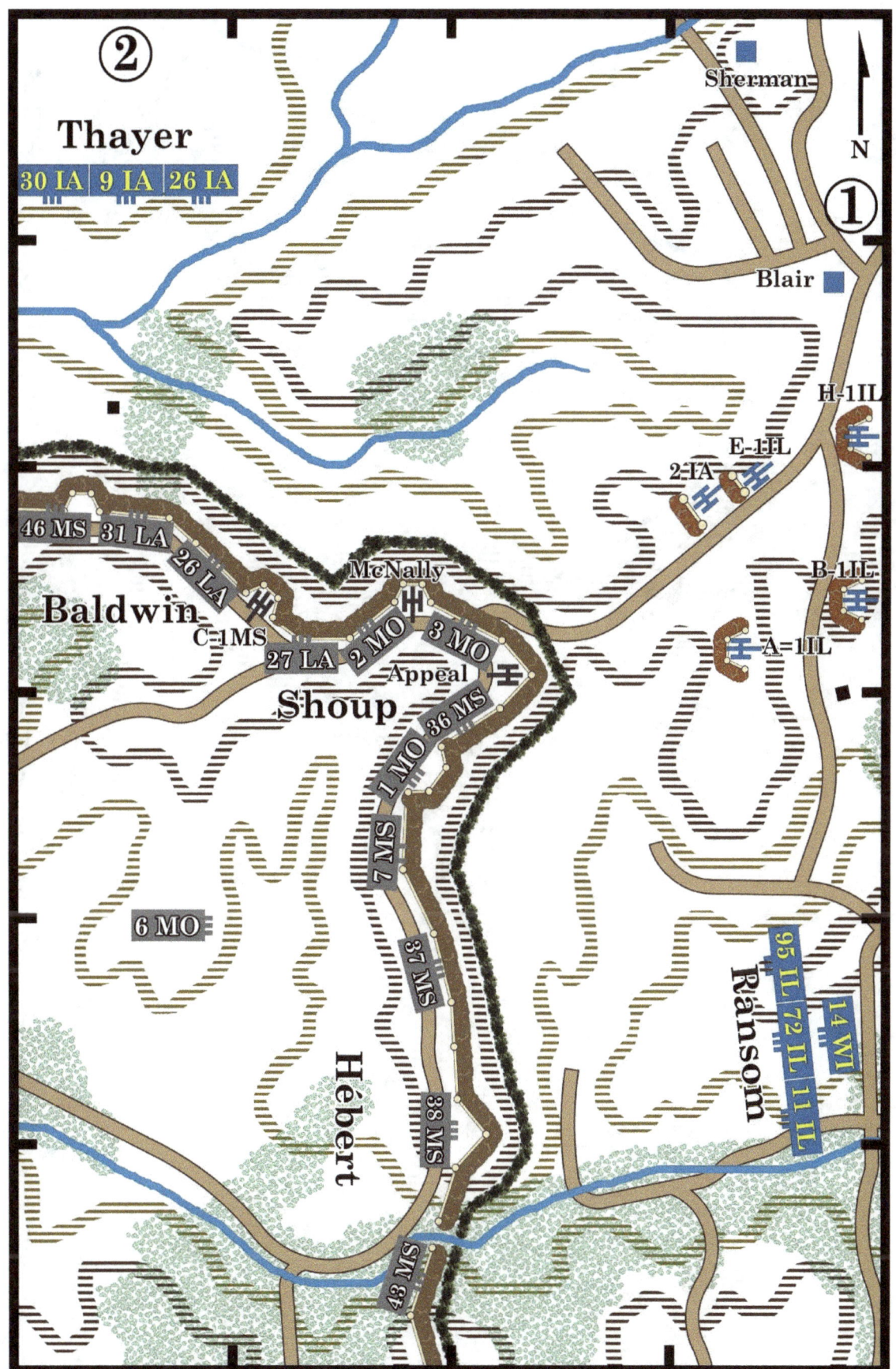

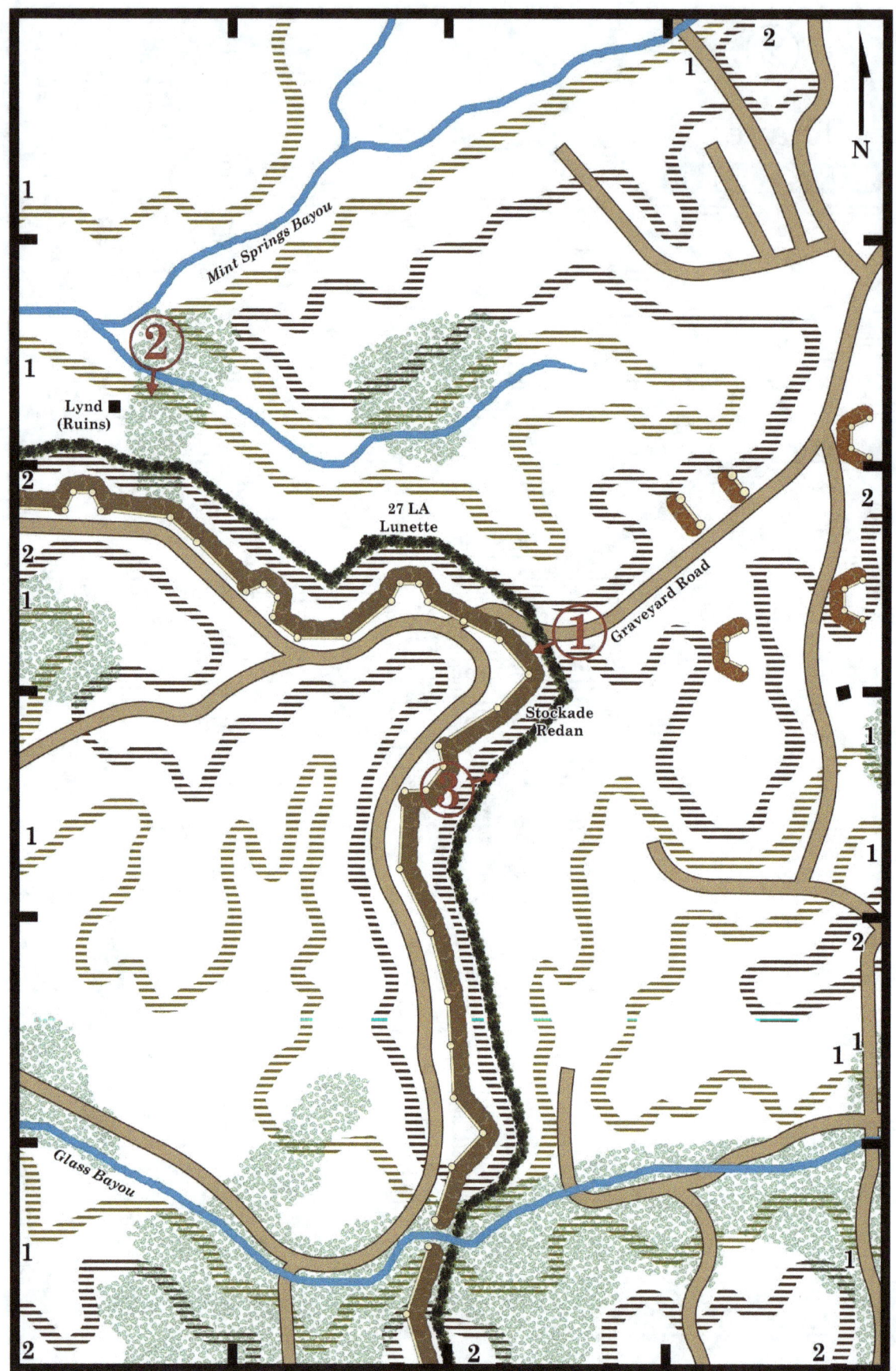

Vicksburg Assault: McPherson May 22nd
May 22nd, 1863

Major General James B. McPherson

Background

The May 22nd attack was an army-wide affair. South of Sherman's attack along the Graveyard Road, Major General James B. McPherson was to storm the works along the Jackson Road, which was the main thoroughfare between Vicksburg and the state capital. Unfortunately, McPherson only had two of his three divisions on the field. It's third had two brigades dispersed in the rear areas, and General Ransom's brigade along Sherman's zone. Still, the remaining divisions were solid veterans who had seen plenty of combat during the war. Brigadier General John A. Logan, who had smashed the Confederates at Champion Hill just a week earlier, would lead the attack down the Jackson Road.

It was a daunting challenge. The road was guarded by two large earthworks. The first was to the left of and immediately straddling the road. It would later be named the 3rd Louisiana Redan after the regiment that was stationed there. To the right of the road was a stout bastion sitting on the highest ground on the Confederate line, termed the Great Redoubt, or Fort Hill by the Union. The line was studded with lunettes and redoubts housing artillery and infantry, facing clear fields of fire looking down into deep ravines.

After an artillery bombardment, the attack began on time at 10 o'clock in the morning. Like the Graveyard Road to the north, Logan had is lead brigade storm the redoubt in front in march column, with the plan to deploy off the road right in front of the works. The plan mostly succeeded, but the firepower from the redoubt was just too much, and the height and strength of the terrain and parapet was just too tall. The Federal soldiers could make no headway. With the two lead regiments stalled, the remainder of the lead brigade sought cover, and with this the rest of the division stopped.

To the south, Brigadier General John D. Stevenson's brigade rushed up the steep hill to climb the Great Redoubt. His men did a brave and admiral job, with the Irish 7th Missouri planting their green flag on the slope of the redoubt. Confederate division commander Major General John H. Forney, in the Great Redoubt, marveled at their bravery. But the return fire from front and flank was just too much for human endurance. Soon, Stevenson's men came tumbling down the slope to find what cover they could until dark. The remaining two brigades in the division decided they could not storm the works in their sector, so didn't even make the attack. They would be sent to help McClernand during the renewed attacks at 2:00 p.m., where one commander would be killed and they still failed. The Confederate center held.

Game Overview

The second of the May 22nd grand assault scenarios. This is a small corps-sized game where the Union must come up with and hone a good strategy for attacking heavy fortifications. The set-up is a little intense, but it should make a good representation of the actual battle.

The game map is 4' x 5'. The game starts at 9 a.m. and ends when the Union can no longer advance, or the Confederates break and are forced off the board.

This scenario can also be combined with the next McClernand game for a large, massed assault.

Looking from the Union lines toward the Confederates. The Great Redoubt is the obelisk in the center. Part of the ridge along which runs the Jackson Road is to the right.

Terrain

Most of the terrain on the map centers around the long ridge in the center, along which runs the Confederate earthworks and forts. The Jackson Road follows a narrow east-west ridge running perpendicular to the main one. The first level elevations are a light tan color, and the second level are the usual dark brown. The elevations should be a full 1 inch tall, and are rough terrain to cross. The first level elevations in front of the works can provide cover and block line of sight. The second elevations just in front of the works do not. The Confederates should be able to see any attacking unit all the way to the first elevation. Use common sense with line of sight for the ridges and elevations along the Jackson Road. For simplicity, you can also leave off the first level of elevation and just use one tall elevation along the main works and Jackson Road.

The Confederate trenches are heavy works. In front of them is a line of felled trees and obstacles in an abatis. Most rules should have their own built in mechanics for negotiating the difficulties in crossing both obstacles. It may seem unrealistic to have open terrain between the two elevation levels, but if you abstract the rough terrain of the slopes themselves, and the combined obstacles of the abatis and heavy works, it should all balance out. The 3rd Louisiana can spread out in the same, main redan in which the Appeal Battery is deployed. The trench line on the right side of the Jackson Road should have a small traverse protecting it from flanking fire down the main road.

Glass Bayou is rough terrain to cross, but the smaller streams on the rest of the board only deduct and inch from movement. The woods are open for visibility, and only subtract and inch from movement. The Union batteries are behind medium works.

Deployment

Begin the game with the units on the board as depicted on the scenario map. The Union may begin laying prone. The two assault regiments in Brigadier General John E. Smith's brigade are far enough behind the lines to avoid pass through fire or casualties. General Logan begins with Smith's brigade.

The game begins at 9 a.m. with an artillery bombardment by the Union guns. The Union

Major General John H. Forney

regiments must remain in place. The infantry are released at 10 a.m. on Turn [7/5/4]. Generals Grant and McPherson enter the board at **1** on Turn [2/2/2]. Grant may elect to remain off the board if he wishes.

The Confederate infantry can spread out to fill more space, and the twists and turns of the lunette and redans, if the rules allow them to without penalties. The artillery is deployed by single sections of two guns each. The 6th Missouri Infantry enters at **2** on Turn [14/10/8]. General Forney begins the game in the Great Redoubt. General Hébert is with the 3rd Louisiana. The Confederate are not constrained by the artillery bombardment, and may move freely on Turn [1/1/1].

Victory Conditions

The game continues until the Confederates are forced from the board, or the Union can no longer advance using the command and control rules being played.

Order of Battle

Army of the Tennessee
MG Ulysses S. Grant [+2]

Seventeenth Army Corps
MG James B. McPherson [+2]

Third Division
BG John A. Logan [+2]

1st Brigade BG John E. Smith [+1]	ES 1,655	20 83	30 55	40 41	50 33	100 17	Status	Arm.
20th Illinois	212	11	7	5	4	2	3	R
31st Illinois	353	18	12	9	7	4	3	R
45th Illinois	299	15	10	7	6	3	3	R
124th Illinois	459	23	15	11	9	5	3	R
23rd Indiana	333	17	11	8	7	3	3	R

2nd Brigade BG Mortimer D. Leggett [+1]	ES 1,463	20 73	30 49	40 37	50 29	100 15	Status	Arm.
30th Illinois	334	17	11	8	7	3	3	R
20th Ohio	401	20	13	10	8	4	3	R
68th Ohio	389	19	13	10	8	4	3	R
78th Ohio	339	17	11	8	7	3	3	R

The point of the 3rd Louisiana Redan looking down the Jackson Road toward the Union lines.

3rd Brigade BG John D. Stevenson [+1]	ES	20	30	40	50	100	Status	Arm.
	2,165	108	72	54	43	22		
8th Illinois	353	18	12	9	7	4	3	R
17th Illinois	345	17	12	9	7	3	3	R
81st Illinois	481	24	16	12	10	5	3	R
7th Missouri	392	20	13	10	8	4	3	R
32nd Ohio	595	30	20	15	12	6	3	R

Seventh Division

BG Isaac F. Quimby [+1]

1st Brigade Col. John B. Sanborn [+1]	ES	20	30	40	50	100	Status	Arm.
	1,516	76	51	38	30	15		
48th Indiana	314	16	10	8	6	3	3	R
59th Indiana	554	28	18	14	11	6	3	R
4th Minnesota	385	19	13	10	8	4	3	R
18th Wisconsin	263	13	9	7	5	3	3	R

The Great Redoubt looking down into the ravine towards Stevenson's attack.

2nd Brigade	ES	20	30	40	50	100	Status	Arm.
Col. Samuel A. Holmes [+1]	1,321	66	44	33	26	13		
56th Illinois	304	15	10	8	6	3	3	R
17th Iowa	304	15	10	8	6	3	3	R
10th, 24th Missouri	304	15	10	8	6	3	3	R
80th Ohio	408	20	14	10	8	4	3	R

3rd Brigade	ES	20	30	40	50	100	Status	Arm.
Col. George B. Boomer [+1]	1,334	67	44	33	27	13		
93rd Illinois	398	20	13	10	8	4	3	R
5th, 10th Iowa	598	30	20	15	12	6	3	R
26th Missouri	338	17	11	8	7	3	3	R

Artillery Battalion	ES	Status	Armament
Cpt. Frank C. Sands [+1]			
11th Ohio Battery		3	**2x** 6 lb. JR, **2x** 6 lb. SB, **2x** 12 lb. H
6th Wisconsin Battery		3	**2x** 6 lb. JR, **2x** 6 lb. SB, **2x** 12 lb. H
12th Wisconsin Battery		3	**4x** 10 lb. P

Thirteenth Army Corps
Tenth Division

Artillery Battalion	ES	Status	Armament
17th Ohio Battery		3	**2x** 10 lb. P

Army of Vicksburg

Smith's Division

Baldwin's Brigade	ES	20	30	40	50	100	Status	Arm.
17th Louisiana	388	19	13	10	8	4	3	R

Shoup's Brigade	ES	20	30	40	50	100	Status	Arm.
29th Louisiana	472	24	16	12	9	5	3	R

Artillery	ES	Status	Armament
Tobin's Tennessee Battery		3	**2x** 6 lb. JR, **2x** 24 lb. H

Forney's Division
MG John H. Forney [+2]

Hébert's Brigade	ES	20	30	40	50	100	Status	Arm.
BG Louis Hébert [+1]	1,703	85	57	43	34	17		
3rd Louisiana	477	24	16	12	10	5	4	R
21st Louisiana	425	21	14	11	9	4	2	R
38th Mississippi	368	18	12	9	7	4	3	M
43rd Mississippi	433	22	14	11	9	4	3	M

Moore's Brigade	ES	20	30	40	50	100	Status	Arm.
BG John C. Moore [+1]	1,473	74	49	37	29	15		
40th Alabama	523	26	17	13	10	5	2	R
35th Mississippi	488	24	16	12	10	5	3	R
40th Mississippi	462	23	15	12	9	5	3	R

Looking up from Stevenson's brigade's approach towards the Great Redoubt.

Artillery	ES	Status	Armament
Co. C, 1st Mississippi Artillery		3	**2x** 6 lb. SB
Co. C, 2nd Alabama Bn.		3	**2x** 6 lb. SB
Appeal's Arkansas Battery		3	**2x** 3" R
Co. B, Point Coupee Artillery		3	**2x** 3" R
Sengstak's Alabama Battery		3	**2x** 6 lb. SB

Bowen's Division
MG John S. Bowen [+2]

First Brigade	ES	20	30	40	50	100	Status	Arm.
6th Missouri	252	13	8	6	5	3	4	R

Second Brigade	ES	20	30	40	50	100	Status	Arm.
BG Martin E. Green [+1]	871	44	29	22	17	9		
19th, 20th, 21st Arkansas	321	16	11	8	6	3	3	R
1st AR Cavalry Bn.*. 1st AR SS Bn.	245	12	8	6	5	2	3	R
1st, 3rd Missouri Cavalry*	305	15	10	8	6	3	4	R

Artillery	ES	Status	Armament
Landis' Missouri Battery		3	**2x** 24 lb. H

Optional Rules

This game can be combined with the following McClernand Assault scenario to play a grand attack upon the works at Vicksburg. The McPherson map is to the north, the McClernand map to the south. The foot increment grid lines match up exactly, forming a 4' x 11' large map. Unfortunately, the contours of the land make it impossible to line up with Sherman's attack map to form a complete, large scenario for the 22nd.

Author's Notes

The Confederate line here is, if anything, more formidable than confronting Sherman to the north. However, there are more Union brigades deployed from the outset in more favorable starting points. Like the other Vicksburg games, this is a chance to put your game set's heavy works rules to the test to see how well you can break them. Test out different formations. Regimental assault columns. Brigade columns. Supported attacks. Be creative.

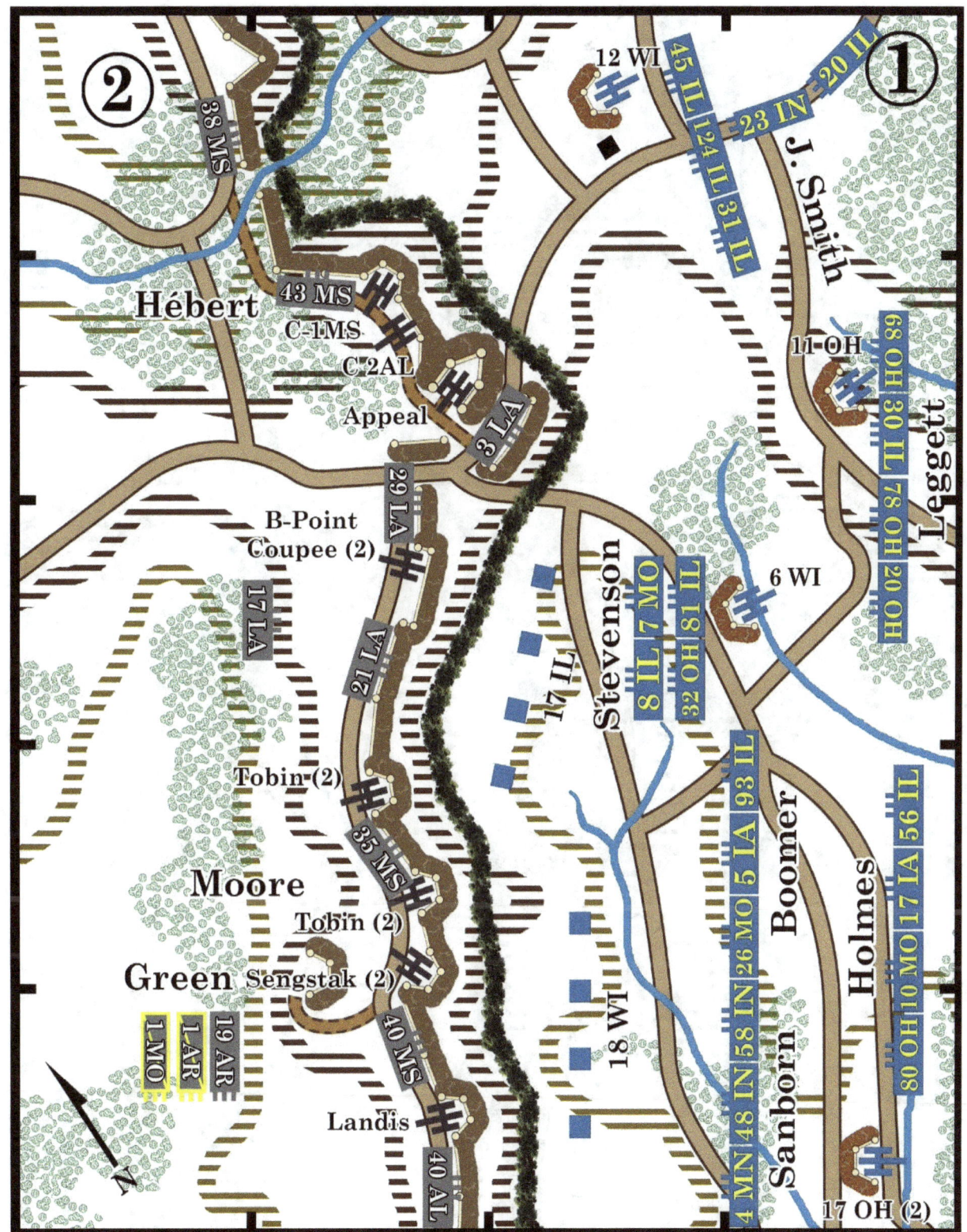

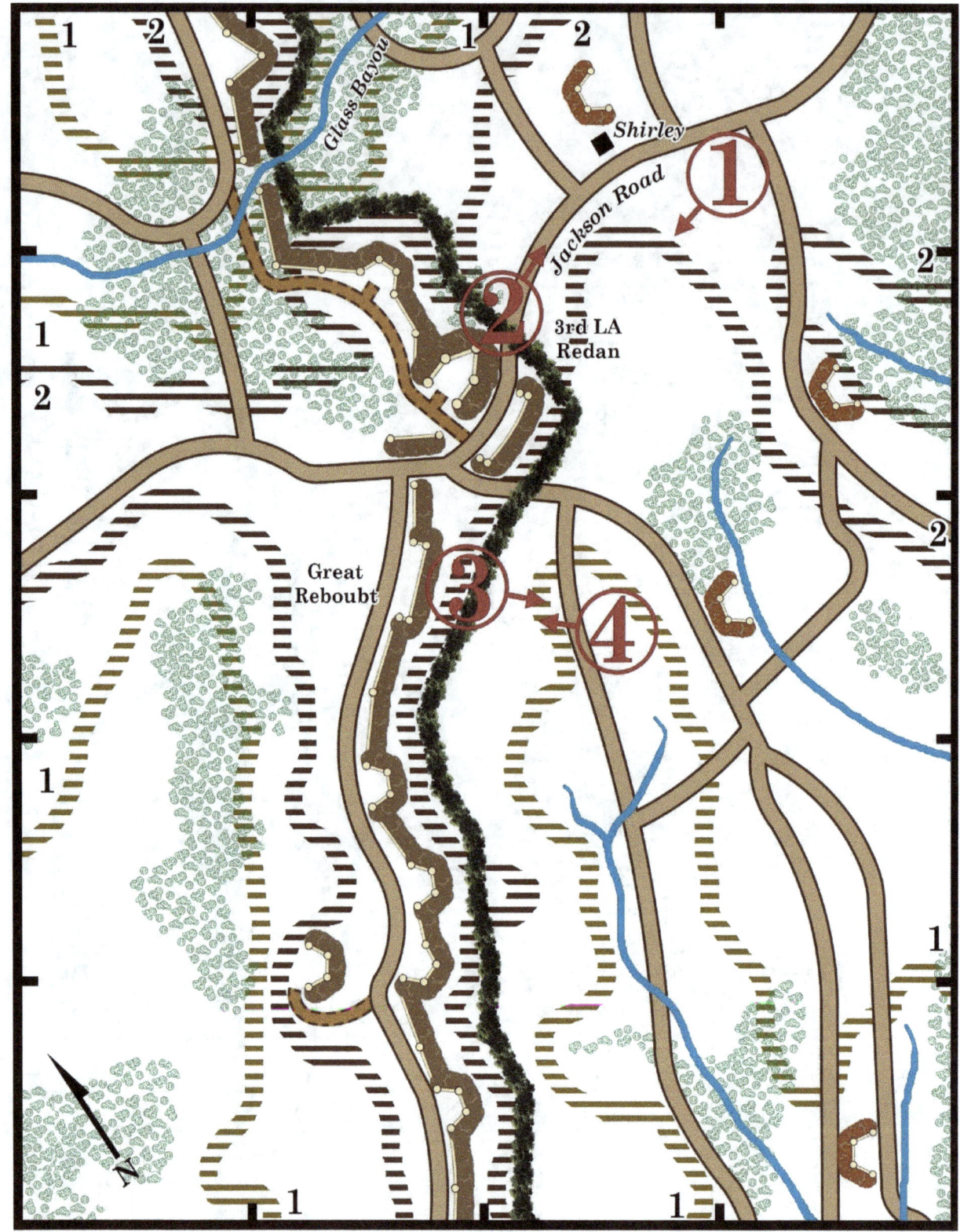

Vicksburg Assault: McClernand May 22nd
May 22nd, 1863

Background

Major General John A. McClernand's Thirteenth Corps held the southern flank of the Army of the Tennessee. They had the farthest to go to deploy along the Vicksburg fortifications opposite the rebels, but managed to get into position in time for the planned May 22nd assault. In some ways, the terrain was a bit easier in this sector. The Baldwin's Ferry Road and Southern Railroad cut through the Confederate lines here, each protected by imposing forts. But south of the railroad the terrain eased a little bit from the deep gullies and ravines. The Confederate trenches were still on high ground, of course, and the slopes were still steep, but maybe not as steep as in front of the Stockade Redan. There were three main forts in front of McClernand. The soon to be named 2nd Texas Lunette guarded the Baldwin's Ferry Road, the appropriately named Railroad Redoubt dominated the Southern Railroad entrance through the lines, and a small work called the Square Fort sat at the limit of the Thirteenth Corps' deployment.

Sherman and McPherson's efforts had relied on a concentration of force on a narrow front, where the reserves could exploit a breakthrough. This tactic had failed with Blair's division in front of the Stockade Redan, and with Logan's division at the 3rd Louisiana Redan. McClernand chose a different way. He would assault with all of his available divisions on line across his entire front. One division each would attack the 2nd Texas Lunette and the Railroad Redoubt, and a third the open space south to the Square Fort. His remaining available brigade would stay in reserve to follow up any success.

The attack began on time at 10 o'clock following the same artillery bombardment along the entire line. The divisions moved forward, but the results were largely the same as the other corps. Command confusion and improper deployments blunted the attacks on the larger forts. The 2nd Texas Lunette held fast, but there was a glimmer of success at the Railroad Redoubt. There Brigadier General Michael K.

Major General John A. McClernand

Lawler's brigade, the same that broke the lines at Big Black River, stormed up the hill and managed to breech the redoubt and gain a small foothold inside. The division to the south, however, made little headway under front and flanking fire from the Square Fort.

McClernand reported the success at the Railroad Redoubt to Grant, but exaggerated its extent and called for the army to renew its efforts to support him. Grant, not wanting to doubt his senior corps commander in the middle of the battle, took him at his word and ordered the army to renew its attacks at 2 p.m. They did so, but only added to the casualty lists. Shuffling of reserves and counterattacks at the Railroad Redoubt pushed the Federals back, and secured control of that fort for the rebels. The day ended with no success anywhere along the lines. McClernand's exaggerated report would be one of the last straws in the relationship between him and Grant. Grant would eventually remove McClernand from command in June.

Grant now realized that the city would not fall quickly. A proper siege would have to begin, which the Union commander started immediately. No more major attacks would be launched at the Confederates. After generous reinforcements, some maneuvering to block a relief army under Joseph E. Johnston at Jackson, and a few mines detonated under the 3rd Louisiana Redan, Pemberton surrendered the city on July 4th.

The view of the Railroad Redoubt from Lawler's attack. The Iowans gained a small foothold at the point of the fortress, but were pushed out later in the afternoon.

Game Overview

The last of the great assaults on Vicksburg for May 22nd. It is another corps sized game, with the focus on piercing the Confederate line and driving them from the table for a quick surrender of the fortress city.

The map is 4' x 6'. The game begins at 9 a.m. and ends when the Union force the Confederates from the board, or the Union can no longer attack.

Terrain

The terrain for this game is a little less foreboding for the Union, but no loss formidable. There are relatively flat avenues of approach along the Baldwin's Ferry Road-Southern Railroad corridor, as well as a connecting ridge in Stephen D. Lee's sector. Still, the works and obstructions are well made and will not be easy. All the elevations are 1" tall and steep, and are rough terrain to traverse. The first level of hills provides cover for attacking units, unless they are directly in front of the abatis. Please use good judgement and common sense. The second level hills, mainly around the Railroad Redoubt and in front of the 37th Alabama, do not provide any cover if they are right in front of Confederate trenches. Use the abatis guidelines for the rules being played.

The streams on the map only take off an inch from movement. They are not the rugged bayous further north. The woods are open woods and only deduct and inch from open movement cost, and are light woods for visibility. The Confederate fortifications are heavy works. The Union artillery lunettes are medium works. The railroad does not affect the game.

Deployment

Set up as shown on the scenario map. The game begins at 9 a.m. with an artillery bombardment from the union batteries. The union infantry may not move. They are released on Turn [7/5/4]. The remaining regiments in Benton's brigade enter in march column on the Baldwin's Ferry Road at **1** on the same Turn [7/5/4]. Burbridge's brigade behind them on Turn [12/8/6]. McClernand can begin the game next to any of the five batteries along the Baldwin's Ferry Road.

If the rules allow it without penalty, the Confederate infantry regiments should spread out

Brigadier General Stephen D. Lee

along the line in all the lunettes and redoubts. General Stevenson begins the game with General Lee, wherever the players decide to place him along his brigade line. The Confederates may move freely starting Turn [1/1/1], during the artillery bombardment. General Green's Brigade arrives at **2** in march column on Turn [16/11/8]. They may be next to each other and not necessarily in a single line.

Victory Conditions

The game continued until the Union can no longer attack or advance because their morale, or command cohesion, is spent. Or they break through and the Confederates are forced off the board.

Order of Battle

Army of the Tennessee

Thirteenth Army Corps
MG John A. McClernand [+2]

Ninth Division
BG Peter J. Osterhaus [+2]

1st Brigade	ES	20	30	40	50	100	Status	Arm.
Col. James Keigwin [+0]	1,504	75	50	38	30	15		
118th Illinois, 69th Indiana	507	25	17	13	10	5	3	R
49th Indiana	338	17	11	8	7	3	3	R
7th Kentucky	357	18	12	9	7	4	3	R
120th Ohio	302	15	10	8	6	3	3	R

2nd Brigade	ES	20	30	40	50	100	Status	Arm.
Col. Daniel W. Lindsey [+0]	1,492	75	50	37	30	15		
22nd Kentucky	272	14	9	7	5	3	3	R
16th Ohio	385	19	13	10	8	4	3	R
42nd Ohio	486	24	16	12	10	5	3	R
114th Ohio	348	17	12	9	7	3	3	R

The parapet of the Railroad Redoubt looking towards the Union lines.

Artillery Battalion	ES	Status	Armament
7th Michigan Battery		3	**6x** 3" R
1st Wisconsin Battery		3	**6x** 20 lb. P

Tenth Division
BG Andrew J. Smith [+2]

1st Brigade	ES	20	30	40	50	100	Status	Arm.
BG Stephen G. Burbridge [+1]	1,189	59	40	30	24	12		
16th, 67th Indiana	524	26	17	13	10	5	3	R
83rd Ohio	318	16	11	8	6	3	3	R
23rd Wisconsin	347	17	12	9	7	3	3	R

2nd Brigade	ES	20	30	40	50	100	Status	Arm.
Col. William J. Landram [+1]	1,413	71	47	35	28	14		
77th Illinois	392	20	13	10	8	4	3	R
130th Illinois	342	17	11	9	7	3	3	R
19th Kentucky	434	22	14	11	9	4	3	R
48th Ohio	245	12	8	6	5	2	3	R

Artillery Battalion	ES	Status	Armament
Chicago Mercantile Battery		3	**2x** 6 lb. SB, **2x** 3" R
17th Ohio Battery		3	**4x** 10 lb. P

Stephen D. Lee's sector of the Confederate line from the Union avenue of approach.

Twelfth Division

BG Alvin P. Hovey [+2]*

*May also benefit the artillery of his own and Osterhaus' Ninth Division.

2nd Brigade Col. William T. Spiceley [+0]	ES	20	30	40	50	100	Status	Arm.
	1,478	74	49	37	30	15		
47th Indiana	392	20	13	10	8	4	3	R
24th Iowa	275	14	9	7	5	3	3	R
28th Iowa	496	25	17	12	10	5	3	R
56th Ohio	316	16	11	8	6	3	3	R

Artillery Battalion	ES	Status	Armament
Battery A, 2nd Illinois	83	3	**2x** 6 lb. JR, **1x** 10 lb. P, **1x** 6 lb. SB
2nd Ohio Battery		3	**4x** 6 lb. JR, **2x** 12 lb. H
16th Ohio Battery		3	**4x** 6 lb. JR, **2x** 6 lb. SB

Fourteenth Division
BG Eugene A. Carr [+2]

1st Brigade	ES	20	30	40	50	100	Status	Arm.
BG William P. Benton [+1]	1,791	90	60	45	36	18		
33rd Illinois	282	14	9	7	6	3	3	R
99th Illinois	437	22	15	11	9	4	3	R
8th Indiana	611	31	20	15	12	6	3	R
18th Indiana	462	23	15	12	9	5	3	R

2nd Brigade	ES	20	30	40	50	100	Status	Arm.
BG Michael K. Lawler [+1]	1,758	88	59	44	35	18		
21st Iowa	433	22	14	11	9	4	4	R
22nd Iowa	536	27	18	13	11	5	4	R
11th Wisconsin	456	23	15	11	9	5	3	M
97th Illinois*	334	17	11	8	7	3	3	R

*Temporarily attached from 2nd Brigade, Tenth Division

Artillery Battalion	ES	Status	Armament
1st Indiana Battery		3	**4x** 6 lb. JR

Army of Vicksburg

Forney's Division

Moore's Brigade	ES	20	30	40	50	100	Status	Arm.
BG John C. Moore [+1]	1,759	88	59	44	35	18		
37th Alabama	403	20	13	10	8	4	3	R
40th Alabama	523	26	17	13	10	5	2	R
42nd Alabama	365	18	12	9	7	4	3	M
2nd Texas	468	23	16	12	9	5	4	R

Artillery	ES	Status	Armament
Co. A, 1st Mississippi Battery		3	**2x** 6 lb. SB, **2x** 12 lb. N
Co. E, 1st Mississippi Battery		3	**2x** 6 lb. SB, **2x** 12 lb. H
Co. B, Point Coupee Artillery		3	**2x** 3" R
Sengstak's Alabama Battery		3	**1x** 3" R, **1x** 24 lb. H

The view of the open ground to the north of the Square Fort from its parapet. The Union attacked from right to left, and the guns in the Square Fort could hit them in the flank.

Stevenson's Division
MG Carter L. Stevenson [+2]

Lee's Brigade	ES	20	30	40	50	100	Status	Arm.
BG Stephen D. Lee [+1]	1,589	79	53	40	32	16		
20th Alabama	358	18	12	9	7	4	3	R
23rd Alabama	285	14	10	7	6	3	3	R
30th Alabama	294	15	10	7	6	3	3	M
31st Alabama	316	16	11	8	6	3	3	R
46th Alabama	336	17	11	8	7	3	3	M

Cumming's Brigade	ES	20	30	40	50	100	Status	Arm.
BG Alfred Cumming [+1]	586	29	20	15	12	6		
34th Georgia	305	15	10	8	6	3	3	R
36th Georgia	281	14	9	7	6	3	3	R

Attached	ES	20	30	40	50	100	Status	Arm.
	500	25	17	13	10	5		
Waul's Texas Legion	500	25	17	13	10	5	2	R

	ES	Status	Armament
Wall's Texas Battery		3	4x 6 lb. SB

Artillery	ES	Status	Armament
Hudson's Mississippi Battery		3	1x 6 lb. SB, 2x 12 lb. H
Waddell's Alabama Battery		3	1x 6 lb. SB, 1x 12 lb. H
Vaiden's Mississippi Battery		3	1x 12 lb. H

Bowen's Division

Second Brigade	ES	20	30	40	50	100	Status	Arm.
BG Martin E. Green [+1]	871	44	29	22	17	9		
19th, 20th, 21st Arkansas	321	16	11	8	6	3	3	R
1st AR Cavalry Bn.* 1st AR SS Bn.	245	12	8	6	5	2	3	R
1st, 3rd Missouri Cavalry*	305	15	10	8	6	3	4	R

Optional Rules

The McPherson and McClernand May 22nd games can be combined into one grand assault. The grid lines on the map match up perfectly to form one large 4' x 11' map.

Author's Notes

The 2nd Texas Lunette and Railroad Redoubt were scenes of intense fighting during the May 22nd attacks. In fact, the Confederates were even able to launch counterattacks on the Union side of the works. The terrain south of the Railroad Redoubt holds some promise, not as steep as the works to the north, but the trenches and lunettes are still dangerous and are filled with infantry and artillery. One curious feature at Vicksburg is that the Confederates deployed their artillery by individual sections of two guns in smaller lunettes, and even in the larger redans and redoubts. By 1864, in the Atlanta Campaign for example, they kept batteries together and dug them in as full batteries for the most part, having learned their lesson on massed firepower.

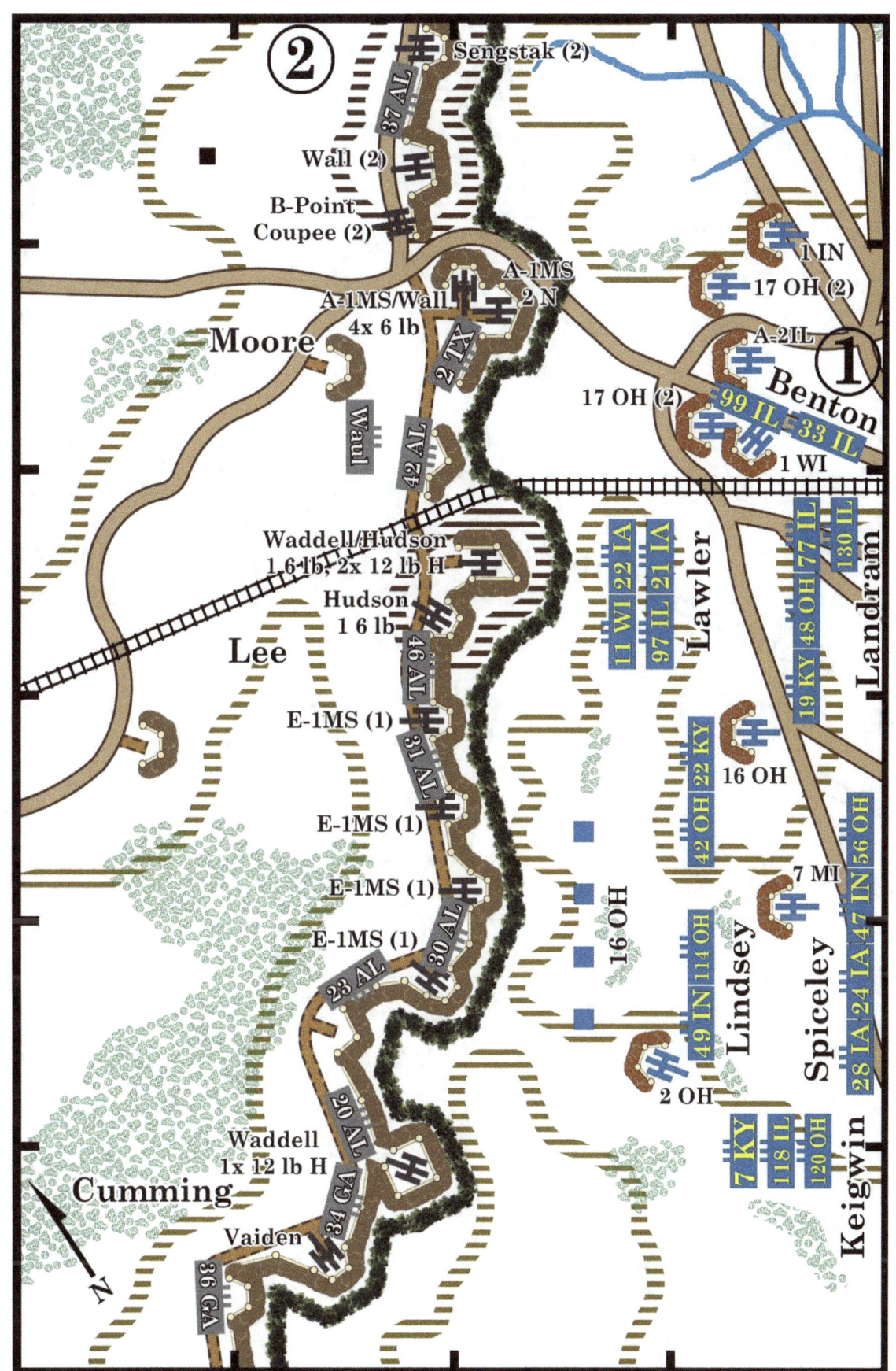

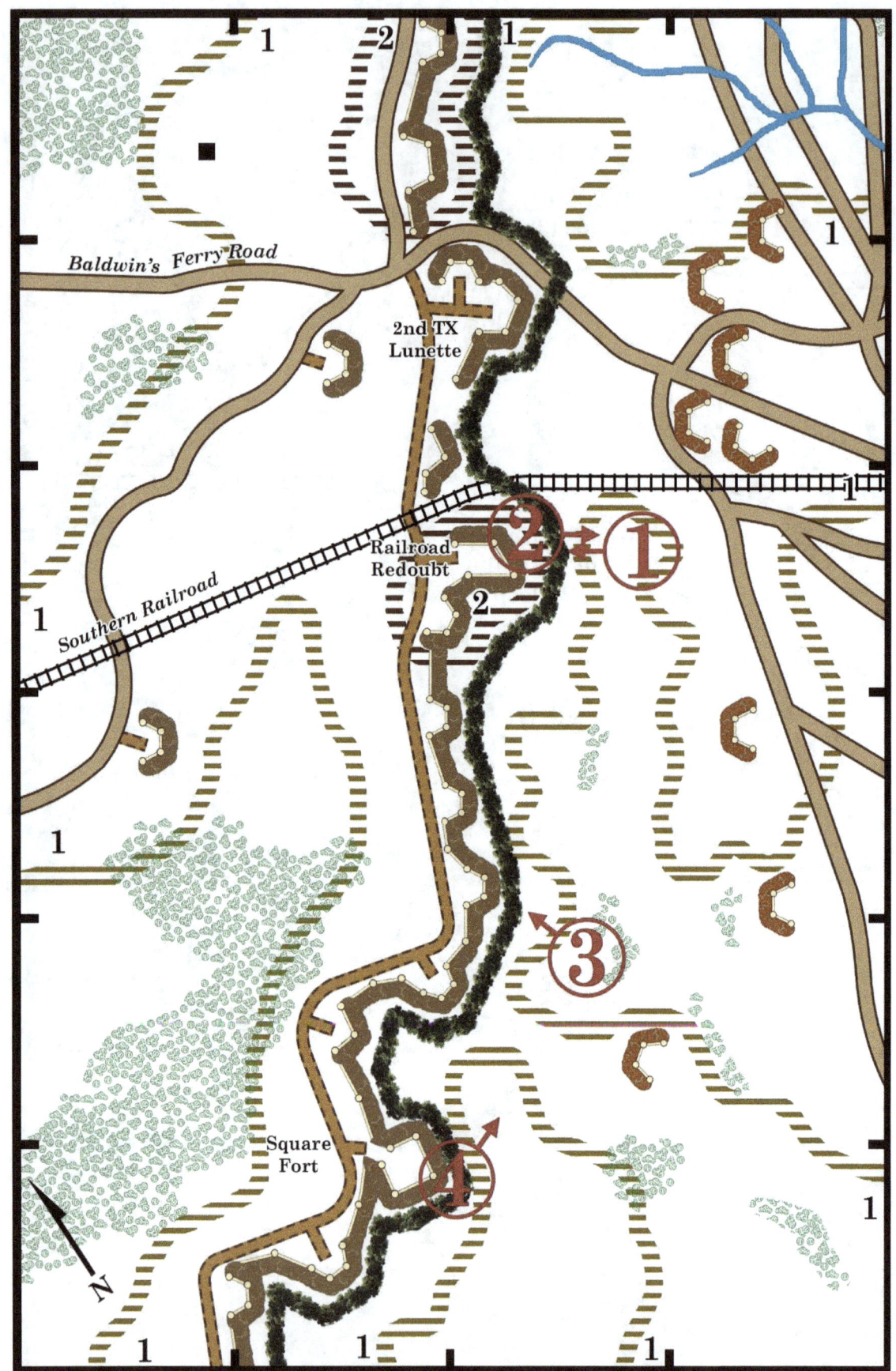

Port Hudson Assault: Northern Flank
May 27th, 1863

Background

By May 1863 General Grant had spent seven months approaching Vicksburg from the north in his attempt to capture the city and re-open the Mississippi River. But another major advance from the *south* was also underway. Major General Nathaniel P. Banks commanded the Army of the Gulf, which was headquartered in New Orleans. It was spread throughout much of southern Florida, Alabama, Texas, and Mississippi, but mostly concentrated in coastal Louisiana and along the southern reaches of the Mississippi. By May 1863 Banks had concentrated his infantry at Baton Rouge and along the Red River at Alexandria. He had five divisions at his disposal, under the umbrella of the Nineteenth Army Corp. His plan was to capture the small town of Port Hudson. Like Vicksburg, the town sat on a hairpin turn of the great river, and high ground on the river bank provide an excellent platform for naval and siege artillery to interdict river traffic. Capturing Port Hudson, along with Vicksburg to the north, would decisively free and open the Mighty Mississippi to the Union once and for all.

The Confederate garrison at Port Hudson was considerably smaller, with only 4,652 present for duty on May 19th. Major General Franklin K. Gardner did the best he could with the forces available. Banks began a slow advance north from Baton Rouge on May 18th with two divisions, and the other three at Alexandria, along the Red River, moved south on the 14th. As Bank's two wings converged on Port Hudson, Gardner fought a small delaying action at Plains Store on May 21st. After being pushed back, the Confederates withdrew into the fortifications encircling the town.

Banks surrounded the town and linked his two forces by the evening of the 22nd. He should have attacked immediately, and was in a position to do so by the evening of the 25th. However, Banks took his time, and Gardner used that time to strengthen his lines. He was expecting an attack from the south, from Baton Rouge, so his lines there were reasonably strong. However,

Brigadier General Godfrey Weitzel

fortifications facing north were practically non-existent. His workshops, gristmill, and cattle were in that area. The brigade guarding this sector, under Colonel Isaiah G. W. Steedman, worked hard to build trenches and lunettes for men and artillery, but they were not complete by the time the Federals attacked.

That attack came on the morning of May 27th. With five divisions in the corps, Banks split his forces into two wings. The left wing was commanded by Brigadier General Godfrey Weitzel, and his attack would focus on the northern end of the Confederate line where it bent back from north-south to east-west. Here Gardner was most vulnerable, with half-finished works. However, the terrain favored the defenders. Big Sandy Creek cut across the front of his lines, and its valley was chocked full of underbrush and debris, which would effectively slow down the advancing enemy and keep them in the kill zone longer. In addition, once Weitzel's advance began the distance they had to travel to make contact, the up and down nature of the ravines, and the oppressive heat sapped the attacker's strength, and more importantly, their will to continue. Few whole or intact units made it across Big Sandy Creek and advanced to the Confederate parapet's themselves, incomplete as they were. Worn out, worn down, and under fire from infantry and cannon, they simply could not break through.

Modern view of the eastern corner of Fort Desperate.

Things looked a little more promising on the flanks. To the west, the brigade of African-American soldiers under Colonel John A. Nelson took a side road that entered Port Hudson along the river. They ran into the 39th Mississippi and a battery of cannon blocking their way. A brave, headlong charge against the works failed to dislodge them, and they fell back. To the east, three brigades converged on a small fort overlooking Little Sandy Creek. This fort stuck out from the main Confederate lines because the garrison's only grist mill for food was located in the valley below, which could not remain unguarded or easily abandoned without a fight. It was manned by the 15th Arkansas and two cannon. Weitzel's men moved into contact with support from most of the wing's artillery. They knocked out the rebel cannon, but even overwhelming numbers could not pry the Arkansans from the fort. Strong Confederate artillery fire from Commissary Hill on the other side of the valley helped slow them down as well. The Union attack faltered, and the fort was renamed Fort Desperate.

Banks would have to hope that attacks elsewhere along the line produced more success.

Game Overview

This is a corps-sized battle, but in truth the Union brigades aren't that large. The terrain and setting up the battlefield are more imposing than the number of units. Still, it should be able to be played in one setting, though it may be a longer game.

The map is 5' x 8'. The battle begins at 7:30 a.m. and ends when the Confederates are forced from the board, or the Union can no longer advance.

Terrain

The terrain is the Confederate key to slowing the Union and hopefully winning the game. The high ground around Port Hudson is cut by Big Sandy Creek and its tributaries. Each level should be ½ inch high, but they are steep. Visit the modern park in person, and you will see that they are virtually cliffs, even compared to the slopes at Vicksburg. The level one slopes can be used as cover by attacking forces. They are a lighter brown color. However, the darker brown level 2 slopes that are *immediately* in front of

Colonel Isaiah G. W. Steedman

Confederates works do not. The rebels have a clear line of sight down the elevation. Use common sense. For example, the level 2 elevations that are several inches away from the front of the 1st Alabama, or the spur in front of Watson's Battery north of the Ambrose house *would* provide cover. Those in front of the 39th Mississippi, 9th Louisiana, or Fort Desperate would not.

The woods are slightly different for this map. The light woods are standard woods or broken terrain, and are light woods for visibility. The darker woods are situated in the low ground and ravines of Big and Little Sandy Creeks. These darker woods are actually brush, scrub, and fallen debris with a scattering of a few copses of upright tree scattered here and there. These are rough terrain. This is going to slow down movement considerably, and the game as well. But it is necessary to accurately depict what the Union had to push through to attack, and give the Confederates a chance to survive. This scrub does not block line of sight, but it does give a small cover bonus (the smallest possible) to any unit inside it.

The creeks in the game are rough terrain. Since most are in the dark woods/scrub anyway, it's all going to be rough terrain. The swamp is rough terrain as well. Fences deduct an inch from movement. The village of Port Hudson isn't built up on the map, but feel free to add some more fences to enclose the houses there. The Confederate fortifications are a mix of heavy, medium, and hasty works. The two batteries on Commissary Hill have a clear line of sight across Little Sandy Creek and into the flanks of Fort Desperate. The railroad does not have any terrain value and does not affect the game.

Deployment

Start the game set up as shown. General Weitzel and the artillery brigade enter at **1** on Turn [10/7/5]. If the Union players wish, they can designate any number of batteries to enter at **2** (in the clearing or along the road) instead by delaying them until Turn [13/9/7]. Colonel Nelson and his Native Guards, along with one section of 12 per howitzers from the 6th Massachusetts Battery, enter along the road at **3** in line of battle on Turn [16/11/8].

The Union have two morale levels in the Order of Battle. For the standard game, use the morale level to the left. This represents the exhaustion, exertion, and heat casualties incurred from the morning march through terrible terrain just to get to the high ground overlooking Big Sandy Creek. Many of these regiments are green and have never seen combat before, and their exhaustion makes things worse. The morale level to the right, in parentheses, is used for the Optional Rules listed in that section.

For the Confederates, General Steedman starts the game at the Ambrose house. General Gardner is in Port Hudson. General Beal is along his lines near the railroad. The 14th and 23rd Arkansas enter as reinforcements along the road at **4** on Turn [13/9/7]. There are a few single guns along the lines. If the rules call for the minimum artillery unit to be a two gun section, then increase it to one section. The gun in River Battery II is on a barbette, and has a 360 degree field of fire. It is still obstructed by houses, however. But it should have an open view of the swamp and up the road to **3**.

Victory Conditions

The battle ends when the Confederates are forced from the board, or the Union can no longer advance. There are no Victory Points to award. The Confederates either stay and hold fast against the Federals, or they are pushed back and lose.

Order of Battle

Army of the Gulf
Nineteenth Army Corps

Right Wing
BG Godfrey Weitzel [+1]

Dwight's Division
BG William Dwight [+1]

1st Brigade, 4th Division	ES	20	30	40	50	100	Status	Arm.
Col. Jacob Van Zandt [+0]	1,576	79	53	39	32	16		
1st Louisiana (US)	669	33	22	17	13	7	1(2)	R
91st New York	488	24	16	12	10	5	1(2)	R
131st New York	419	21	14	10	8	4	1(2)	M

2nd Brigade, 1st Division	ES	20	30	40	50	100	Status	Arm.
Col. Stephen Thomas [+0]	965	48	32	24	19	10		
12th Connecticut	483	24	16	12	10	5	2(3)	R
75th New York	482	24	16	12	10	5	2(3)	R

Native Guard	ES	20	30	40	50	100	Status	Arm.
Col. John A. Nelson [+0]	1,248	62	42	31	25	12		
1st Louisiana Native Guards	607	30	20	15	12	6	1(2)	R
3rd Louisiana Native Guards	642	32	21	16	13	6	1(2)	R

Artillery Battalion	ES	Status	Armament
1st Maine Light Artillery		3	**6x** 6 lb. JR
2nd Massachusetts Battery		3	**6x** 6 lb. JR
6th Massachusetts Battery	108	3	**2x** 12 lb. N, **2x** 12 lb. H
Battery A, 1st United States	100	3	**4x** 12 lb. N, **2x** 3" R
Battery F, 1st United States		3	**6x** 12 lb. N

Photo of the Confederate lines just after the close of the siege. The view is from the Union lines looking over either Big or Little Sandy Creek towards the Confederates works in the background. It gives a good view of the broken terrain and the undergrowth in the valley.

3rd Division
BG Halbert E. Paine [+1]

2nd Brigade Col. Hawkes Fearing [+1]	ES 1,210	20 61	30 40	40 30	50 24	100 12	Status	Arm.
8th New Hampshire	298	15	10	7	6	3	2(3)	R
173rd New York	425	21	14	11	9	4	2(3)	R
4th Wisconsin	487	24	16	12	10	5	1(2)	R

3rd Brigade Col. Oliver Gooding [+1]	ES 1,488	20 74	30 50	40 37	50 30	100 15	Status	Arm.
31st Massachusetts	524	26	17	13	10	5	1(2)	R
38th Massachusetts	398	20	13	10	8	4	2(3)	R
53rd Massachusetts	566	28	19	14	11	6	1(2)	R

Right Center (4th Division)
BG Cuvier Grover [+2]

2nd Brigade BG William K. Kimball [+1]	ES 728	20 36	30 24	40 18	50 15	100 7	Status	Arm.
24th Connecticut	346	17	12	9	7	3	2(3)	R
12th Maine	382	19	13	10	8	4	2(3)	R

This is a photo taken shortly after the siege looking from the Confederate works towards the Union lines. Again, a good shot of the rough terrain, scrubs, and trees in the valley of either Big or Little Sandy Creeks.

3rd Brigade	ES	20	30	40	50	100	Status	Arm.
BG Henry W. Birge [+1]	1,065	53	36	27	21	11		
13th Connecticut	474	24	16	12	9	5	2(3)	R
25th Connecticut	263	13	9	7	5	3	2(3)	R
159th New York	328	16	11	8	7	3	2(3)	R

Department of Mississippi & East Louisiana

District of East Louisiana
MG Franklin A. Gardner [+2]

Left Wing	ES	20	30	40	50	100	Status	Arm.
Col. Isaiah G. W. Steedman [+1]	1,599	80	53	40	32	16		
1st Alabama, 1st Mississippi	504	25	17	13	10	5	3	M(f)
39th Mississippi	342	17	11	9	7	3	3	R
10th, 15th Arkansas	365	18	12	9	7	4	3	M
9th Louisiana Partisan Ranger Bn., Claiborne's Light Infantry	388	19	13	10	8	4	3	R

Center	ES	20	30	40	50	100	Status	Arm.
BG William N. R. Beall [+1]	1,431	72	48	36	29	14		
49th Alabama	376	19	13	9	8	4	3	R
12th Arkansas	328	16	11	8	7	3	3	Sh
14th, 18th Arkansas	416	21	14	10	8	4	3	R
23rd Arkansas	311	16	10	8	6	3	3	M

Artillery Battalion	ES	Status	Armament
Company B, 1st Mississippi Artillery		3	**4x** 6 lb. SB, **2x** 12 lbs. H
Company F, 1st Mississippi Artillery		3	**2x** 6 lb. SB
1st Tennessee Light Artillery		3	**2x** 12 lb. BR, **1x** 24 lb. Rifle[a]
Co. A, 1st Alabama		3	**2x** 24 lb. Rifle[a]
Watson's Louisiana Battery		3	**2x** 6 lb. SB, **2x** 12 lb. H
Co. K, 39th Mississippi		3	**1x** 2 lb. Hughes Rifle[b]
Detachment, 9th LA Partisan Rangers		3	**2x** 2 lb. Hughes Rifle[b,c]
River Battery II		3	**1x** 42 lb. SB

[a] Use rules for a 20 lb. Parrott rifle, with perhaps an slight, extra bonus.

[b] Use rules for a Williams Gun, without any penalties for crippling the gunners, if applicable.

[c] The 9th Louisiana detachment could have actually been Williams Guns instead of Hughes.

Optional Rules

One optional rules is to disregard the lower morale designations and use their "normal" morale for the scenario. This will give the Union a decided edge in a game where they already have the advantage, so think carefully when deciding to use this.

Author's Notes

Banks should have been able to roll over his much weaker opponent on May 27th. Yet he delayed his attack an additional day when he didn't have to, and even then, didn't begin the day as close to the Confederates lines as possible. This broke up his units and further eroded morale. While he did have a core of experience regiments that fought at such places as Fort Bisland and Irish Bend, most of his men had never seen a major battle. Still, the Confederates player is going to be *very* hard pressed to win. They will need to hit the exhausted Union regiments with anything they can to induce morale checks or similar to stop the blue wave.

This game also has some interesting and unique weapons, such as the Hughes rifles, and possibly some Williams Guns. Not to mention some 24 lb. rifles.

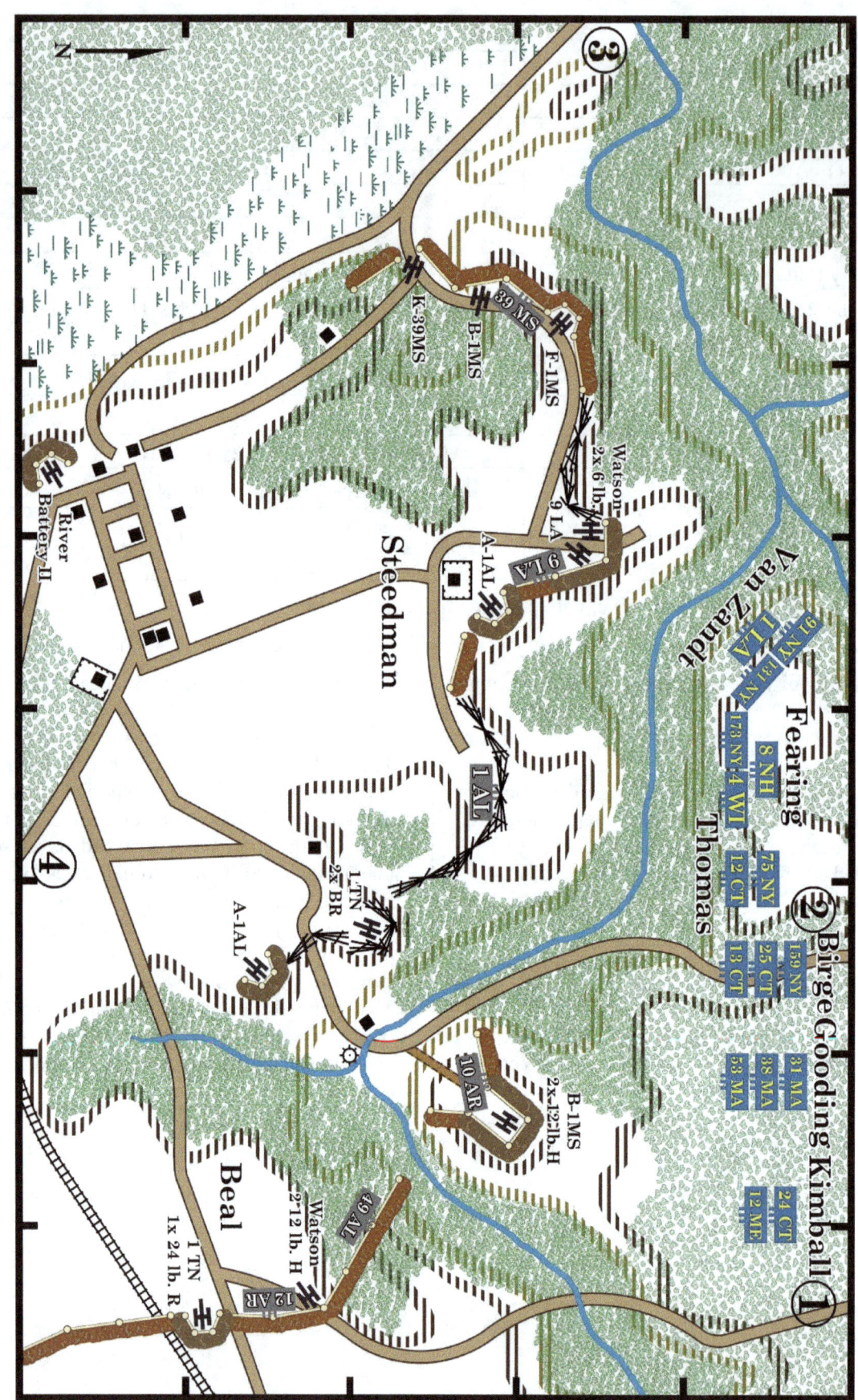

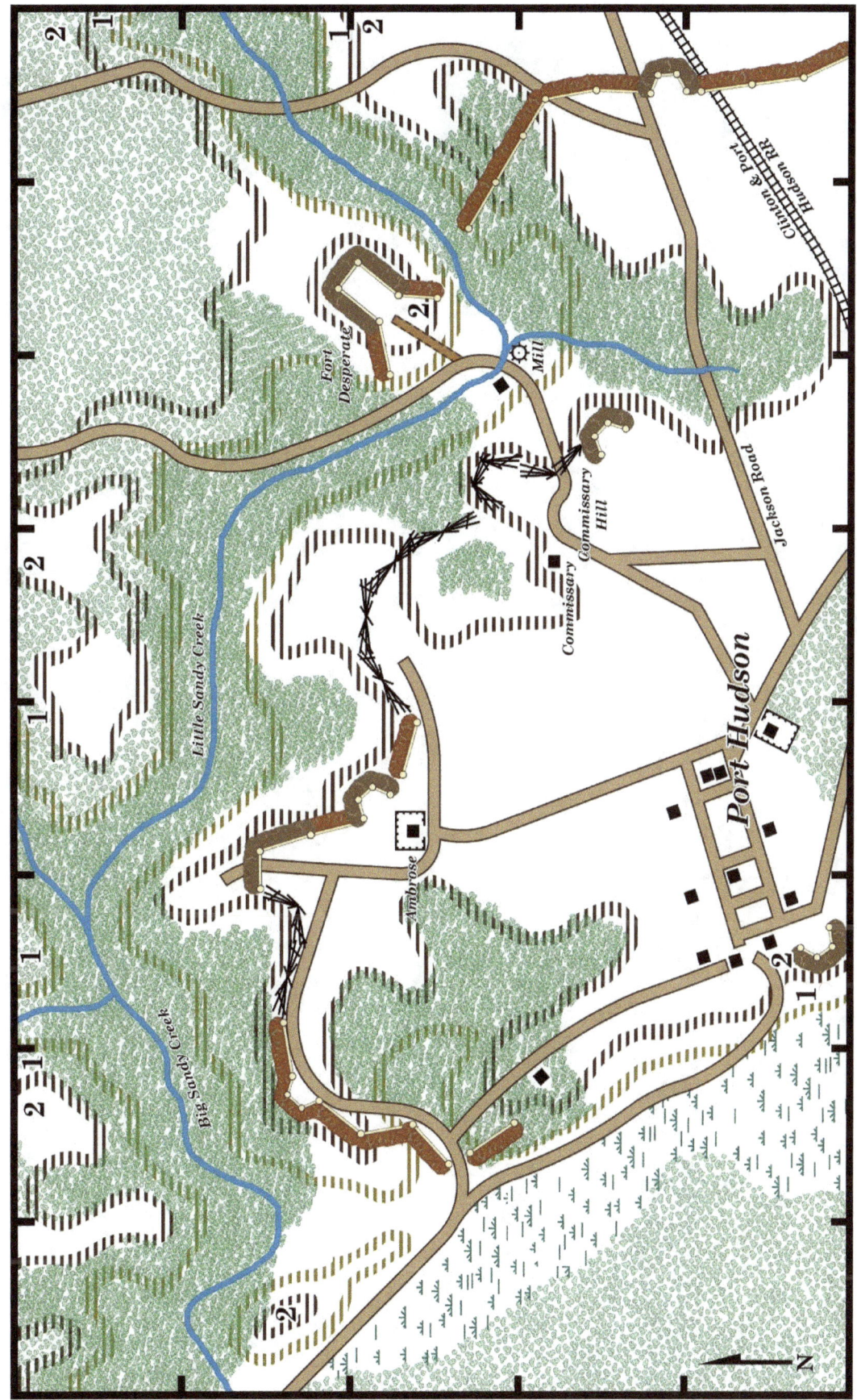

Port Hudson Assault: Eastern Flank
May 27th, 1863

Background

As the fighting raged to the north of Port Hudson, General Banks waited to hear the sound of fighting from the south end of his line, along the eastern face of the ring of fortifications surrounding the town. There Brigadier General Thomas W. Sherman was supposed to be attacking, and the division to his north would follow suit. Yet, the attack never began. About noon Banks rode to Sherman's headquarters, only to find little activity and the division commander eating lunch. After a heated argument, Banks returned to his headquarters and ordered his chief of staff, Brigadier General George L. Andrews, to relieve Sherman. He would then immediately take command of the division, and begin the attack. When Andrews arrived at the front, Sherman had already formed his men and began the advance, so Andrews demurred on relieving him.

The areas adjacent to this section of the Confederate lines were much more open than those to the north. In Sherman's sector, a large wooded and brush filled ravine restricted movement on his right flank. To his left, the countryside was open, as the Confederate fortifications stretched to the south, then swung southwest to connect to the Mississippi River. While this allowed much better movement for Sherman than it did for Weitzel along Big and Little Sandy Creeks, it also provided the Confederates with a much better field of fire across open ground. The only obstacles for the Union were the William Slaughter plantation, its surrounding fences, and a large cornfield. The open ground between was scattered with brush and uneven gullies before ending in a row of abatis directly in front of the rebel trenches.

Sherman began his advance at 2 o'clock. Confederate artillery immediately opened upon them, wounding Sherman early in the fight, and then Brigadier General Neal S. Dow. The men reached the abatis, only to be met with blistering volleys. The Confederate commander, Colonel

Brigadier General Thomas W. Sherman

Col. William R. Miles, had gathered as many arms as he could before the fight began. Most of his men had three muskets apiece, with orders to discharge them, and then have one man load and one man fire. The Federals walked into a withering firestorm at close range as they tried to cross the clothes-shredding, tangled abatis. Flanking fire from both directions added to the destruction. Almost beyond human endurance, the Union broke and ran. Many of them took shelter in the underbrush and small dips in the land and began sniping at the Confederates. They enjoyed a moderate success, and managed to keep the rebel's heads down below the parapet for much of the day. General Andrews then assumed command of the division near the end of the assault. When night fell, the remaining soldiers left in the open made their way back to friendly lines.

The rebel lines had held, and a quick victory at Port Hudson slipped from Bank's grasp. It would take many long weeks of siege warfare to dislodge the defenders. Only when word reached General Gardner that Vicksburg had fallen on July 4th did he begin negotiations to surrender. On July 9th Port Hudson formally surrendered, and the Mississippi River was finally open once more from Minnesota to the Gulf of Mexico. The month's long campaign was over, and the river was finally free and open, severing the Confederacy in two forever.

View of the Confederate lines along the eastern defenses. This is the type of broken ground encountered by the Sherman's men as they advanced towards Miles.

Game Overview

This is a much smaller assault against works, with only a small two-brigade division on the attack. It's good for a quick game, or to experiment with different techniques to attacking works.

The game map is small, only 3' x 4'. The game starts at 2 p.m. and ends when the Confederates are forced from the board, or the Union can no longer advance.

Terrain

The game board is relatively flat. The big exception is the large gully that wraps around the north and west, and there are also two small hills along the Confederate line. Like the Port Hudson North scenario, the light shaded woods are open woods. They only deduct an inch from movement, and are light woods for visibility. The darker shaded woods are a mix of scrub and brush, mixed in with batches of various trees. This area is rough terrain to cross. It does not block line of sight, but it does provide a cover bonus.

The creek is rough terrain to cross, except at the ford, which only deducts an inch from road movement. The fences only deduct an inch from movement. The cornfield is not very tall in May, so it does not have any effect on the game. Nor does the open, plowed field. The fields shown with the random scattering of trees are broken up by scrub, gullies, and other irregularities. These spaces deduct an inch from movement, and provide a small cover bonus for any unit in them. They do not hinder line of sight.

The Confederate works are medium works, with heavy works for the gun emplacements. They have a line of abatis in front of them.

Deployment

Set the game up as shown. General Sherman is in the middle between his two brigades. On Turn [1/1/1], the 128th New York enters in line of battle immediately behind Dow to complete the brigade column. Likewise, the 165th New

Colonel William R. Miles

York enters on Turn [1/1/1] immediately behind Nickerson as the final regiment in the brigade. If General Sherman becomes a casualty, General Andrews may enter the board along the road at **1 one hour**, or [7/5/4] Turns later to assume division command. This does not preclude any normal rules for elevating Dow or Nickerson to temporary command if the rules allow it.

For the Confederates, Colonel Miles can begin the game anywhere along his line south of the creek. He had scrounged all the rifles and muskets he could from the hospitals and arsenal, and many of his men had three weapons each. To reflect this, Confederate infantry units double any first fire bonus if applicable. If doubling it would seem too powerful, adjust to x1.5 instead. For the artillery, if the minimum unit under the rules is a section of two guns, then bump the 24 lb. rifle up to a section instead of a single gun.

Victory Conditions

The game is a breakthrough or nothing setting. The game ends when the Union are stopped and can no longer advance based on the command and control rules, or they break through and force the Confederates from the field.

Order of Battle

Army of the Gulf

Nineteenth Army Corps

2nd Division

BG Thomas W. Sherman [+2]

BG George L. Andrews [+1]*

*Only if General Sherman becomes a casualty and is permanently removed from the game.

1st Brigade BG Neal S. Dow [+1]	ES 1,849	20 92	30 62	40 46	50 37	100 18	Status	Arm.
26th Connecticut	529	26	18	13	11	5	2	R
6th Michigan	450	23	15	11	9	5	3	R
15th New Hampshire	363	18	12	9	7	4	2	R
128th New York	507	25	17	13	10	5	2	R

3rd Brigade BG Frank S. Nickerson [+1]	ES 1,721	20 86	30 57	40 43	50 34	100 17	Status	Arm.
14th Maine	386	19	13	10	8	4	3	R
24th Maine	427	21	14	11	9	4	2	R
165th New York	350	18	12	9	7	4	2	R
177th New York	558	28	19	14	11	6	2	R

Artillery Battalion	ES	Status	Armament
1st Vermont Battery		3	**5x** 3" R
21st New York Battery		3	**4x** 3" R

Department of Mississippi & East Louisiana

District of East Louisiana

Right Wing	ES	20	30	40	50	100	Status	Arm.
Col. William R. Miles [+1]	766	38	26	19	15	8		
9th Louisiana Bn.	249	12	8	6	5	2	3	R
Miles' Legion	311	16	10	8	6	3	3	R
DeGournay's Bn.*	206	10	7	5	4	2	2	R

*Artillerymen serving as infantry.

Center	ES	20	30	40	50	100	Status	Arm.
	362	18	12	9	7	4		
16th Arkansas	362	18	12	9	7	4	3	R

Artillery Battalion	ES	Status	Armament
Co. K, 1st Mississippi Artillery		3	**6x** 12 lb. H
Co. D, 12th Louisiana Heavy Artillery		3	**1x** 24 lb. R*
Boone's Louisiana Battery		3	**2x** 6 lb. SB

*Treat like a 20 lb. Parrott rifle, with perhaps a slight extra bonus.

Optional Rules

There are no optional rules for this game.

Author's Notes

The game is good for a smaller assault upon enemy works, to contrast between the larger scenarios in the rest of the books. Its good practice, both attacking and defending fortifications.

Unfortunately, this portion of the battlefield contains numerous private farms, as well as utilities. There are no open fields that correspond with their historical equivalents, so there are no modern pictures of the battlefield.

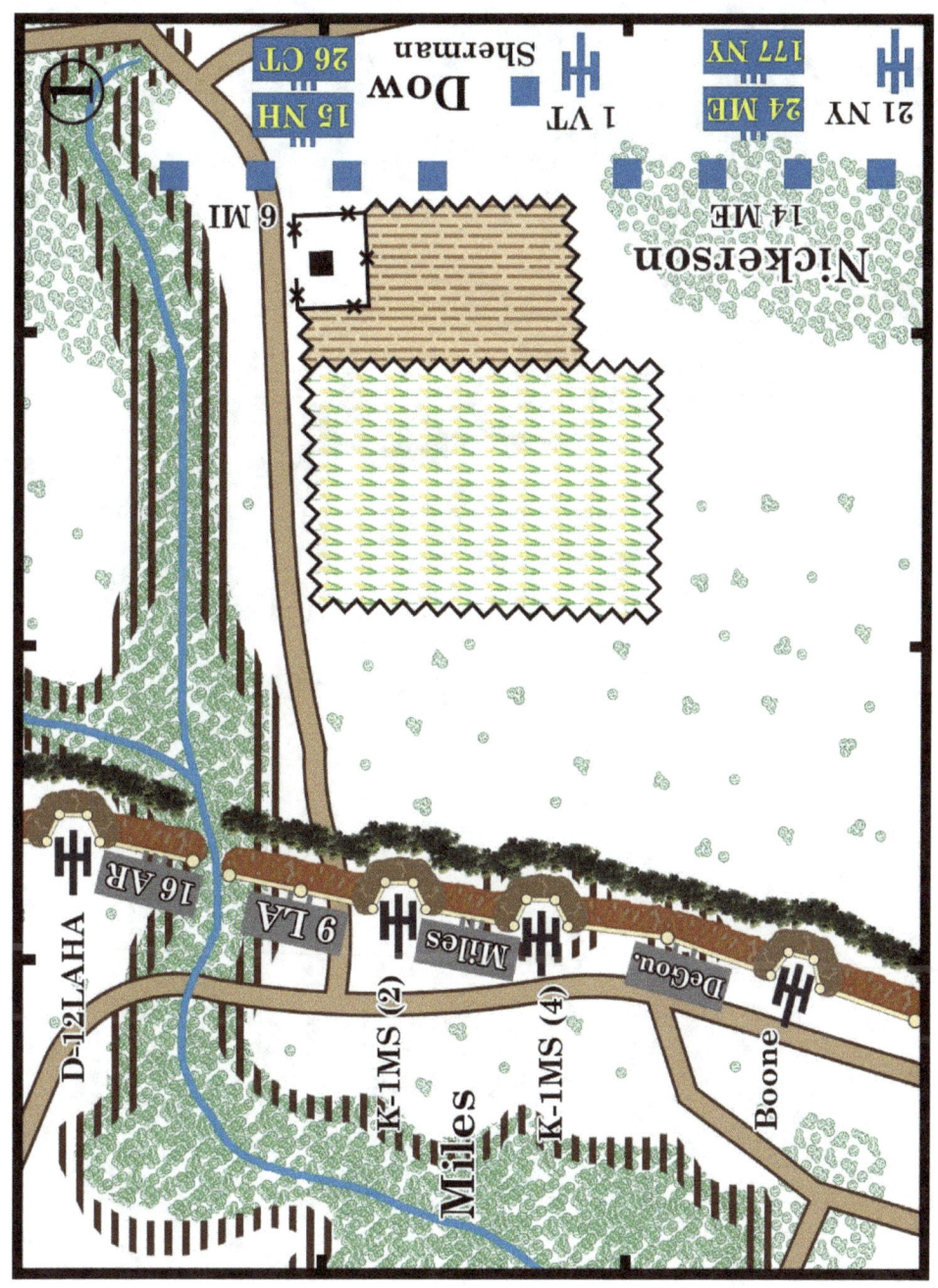

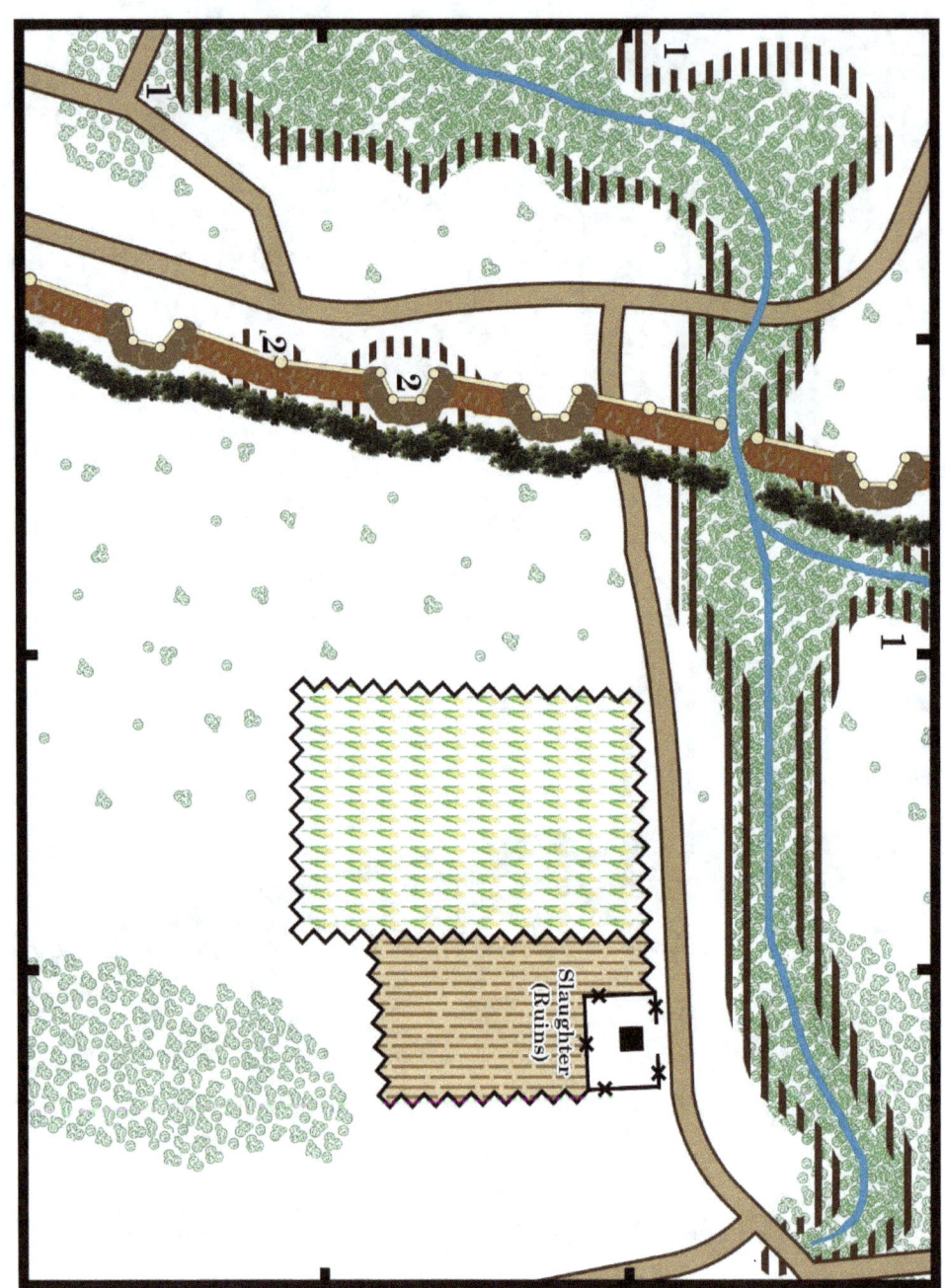

The Battle of Milliken's Bend
June 7th, 1863

Background

General Grant, after the failure of the May 22nd attacks on the Vicksburg fortifications, had no choice but to begin siege operations against the stronghold. What followed were six weeks of digging in front of the city, but also strategic movements to relieve the pressure on the surrounded garrison, if not outright break the siege.

Much of the expectation to save Pemberton was put on the shoulders of General Joseph E. Johnston in Jackson, but a fair amount of pressure was exerted on the Confederate commanders west of the Mississippi River. Major General Richard Taylor was assigned the task of capturing Milliken's Bend. It has been the main supply depot for the Union army at the beginning of the campaign as it marched south along the west bank of the river to the crossing opposite Bruinsburg. Now, however, with the siege underway against the city itself, the main Union supply base had shifted to the Yazoo River near Chickasaw Bayou, scene of the December fighting. The camp at Milliken's Bend was now used to recruit and train escaped slaves and African-American soldiers for service in the Union army.

Taylor occupied Richmond, Louisiana, 17 miles west of Vicksburg, in early June. On June 5th he learned that Milliken's Bend was no longer Grant's main supply base. Still, Taylor planned to clear the Federals from the west bank of the river. He hoped to re-establish communication with the trapped garrison, and maybe even re-open a supply line from the west bank. His main striking power was Major General John G. Walker's Texas Division. Taylor sent Walker on a multi-pronged attack. He sent the 13th Texas Cavalry (Dismounted) to reinforce a raid against the Union outpost at Lake Providence. He dispatched a brigade against a Union garrison at Young's Point, held another brigade in reserve, and sent Brigadier General Henry E. McCulloch to capture Milliken's Bend.

Colonel Hermann Lieb

Colonel Hermann Lieb commanded the camp at Milliken's Bend, and he discovered the build-up of Confederate forces in the area. On June 6th a cavalry and infantry patrol discovered the Confederates north of Richmond. Lieb asked for help, and the gunboat *U.S.S. Choctaw* and the 23rd Iowa were sent to the Bend, arriving during the night. McCulloch used the cooler night to march swiftly to the outpost, and arrived after 2 a.m. The Union outposts and skirmishers soon engaged him. Quickly forming, McCulloch advanced in the growing dawn twilight.

The Union defenders were stationed on a raised levee overlooking the flood plain and a plantation cut by several dense hedges. They had strengthened the levee with cotton bales to form a rough breastwork. As McCulloch's men forced their way through the hedges they spooked a collection of mules used by the garrison. Many of the Federals noted this "moving breastwork" and thought it intentional. As the Texans pushed through the last hedge and reformed, the colored troops fired their first volley, causing much consternation among the rebels. With a yell, the Texans surged forward and up the levee. A vicious hand-to-hand fight began. Lieb's two middle regiments broke, forcing most of his line to fall back through their camps and onto another levee at the river's edge. The 11th Louisiana (African Descent) held onto their corner of the levee to the north.

McCulloch's men attempted to drive the remaining garrison from the second levee and into the river, but the fire from the *Choctaw* discouraged a major attack on this final position. McCulloch sent word back to Walker for reinforcements, and Walker arrived on the scene with the reserve brigade later in the morning. Walker discovered McCulloch's men exhausted from the march, seven hour fight, and 95 degree heat. He would have to attack with the reserve brigade, and he erroneously believed more gunboats had arrived than actually did (only the *U.S.S. Lexington* had appeared to reinforce the *Choctaw*). Walker decided the effort to capture the remaining garrison was not worth the cost in Texas lives, and around noon began his withdrawal back to Richmond. The initial effort to save Vicksburg from the west bank of the river had failed. On the Union side, it showed that black soldiers and former slaves could and would fight, though their contribution was more in surviving than driving back the attackers. Still, it was a propaganda win for the Federals, and coupled with the assault on Fort Wagner by the 54th Massachusetts (Colored) eleven days later, brought the potential of African-American soldiers to the forefront.

Game Overview

This is a small brigade against brigade game. The Union has a good position, but they are outnumbered and inexperienced, even compared to the green Texans who are fighting their first battle as well. Neither has artillery support, except for the Union, but its line of sight is limited. This game can easily be played in one setting.

The board is 2' x 3'. The game begins before dawn at 3:15 a.m. and ends when one side is defeated.

Terrain

The board is flat except for the levees. The levees should be about ¼ inch tall, or ½ inch if necessary. The top should be just wide enough to hold a regiment. The levees deduct an inch from movement. They also block line of sight. Any regiment on top can use them as light works, because the Union has been fortifying them.

The hedges are only about a man's height, and only block line of sight on level ground. Any unit on a levee can see over them easily. They are rough terrain, but should only be wide enough to interrupt movement for one full turn maximum. The small creeks only deduct an inch from movement, if combat happens to reach those far corners. There is some disagreement on the shape of the hasty works built by the 11th Louisiana (African Descent) as an extension of the levee. The red hasty works are an optional configuration. Choose one at the beginning of the scenario, not both.

The Union camps are rough terrain for any formed unit such as a line, assault column, etc., as well as disorder. It is open terrain for skirmishers and march columns, as they can easily navigate the company streets. The Mississippi River is impassable terrain. Treat is as the edge of the board in terms of routing units and dispersal.

Deployment

Start the game as shown on the scenario map. The first few turns are twilight. If your game rules do not have night rules, consider the following.

Twilight
- Visibility in open changes to light woods
- Halve unit firing strengths.

Turn [5/4/3] is the first full daylight turn.

The mules in between the lines should be represented by a single stand with about 4 mule or horse miniatures on it. A cavalry horse holder stand is a good substitute. They will remain stationary unless a unit gets within 1 inch of them. They will then move in the opposite direction from that unit's movement. They move as an infantry line of battle. They are not issued an order and are not controlled by any player. If a unit get within their vicinity, they will simply begin moving, even mid-turn. If they reach a hedge or other obstacle, roll a die and randomly decide a 50% chance which direction they will move. If a unit moves past them and out of their "range," then they will simply stop moving. If they are fired upon and take a "casualty" they will move in the opposite direction from the fire at a bonus, or charge distance rate. If they take a casualty a second turn in a row, they disperse and are removed from the game.

View near the battlefield from atop the modern levee. Today's levee is taller and wider than the 1863 version. This modern view shows the flat terrain and isolated woodlots common in the river floodplain.

The 23rd Iowa only had a small contingent present. They can attach themselves to another regiment at the beginning of the game, most likely the combined 13th Louisiana and 1st Mississippi African Descent regiment. If they do, increase the combined unit's morale to level 2.

Colonel Isaac Shepard was the actual garrison commander, but he was under arrest and could not command the troops. However, he still remained with them, encouraging them. He can use his office bonus for morale purposes, but not command and control, and he cannot give orders to Federal units. He begins the game with the 13th Louisiana African Descent regiment.

The *U.S.S. Choctaw* can only face one direction per turn. That is, it cannot fire one broadside, then turn and fire the other in the same turn. It can move up to one foot per turn, including turning around once. It can fire while moving easily, and does not get a moving penalty for artillery. This isn't a navy game, so keep it simple. The inner levee at the river's edge does block the gunboat's line of sight, but take advantage of any indirect fire rules if they are available, especially with friendly units on the levee spotting for them. If for some ungodly reason the game isn't over by Turn [32/24/18], the *U.S.S. Lexington* arrives at **1** on that turn.

To reflect the animosity between the U.S. colored troops and the Confederates, any time a Union black regiment engages in melee or hand-to-hand combat, add a small casualty bonus. Depending on the rules, it could be a +1 to a die roll, or a shift up one column. Please note, this is not a "racial bonus." This applies to both sides, and reflects the savage close combat described by both participants. In the real battle, they fought viciously. Several Union white officers that were captured leading the black regiments were later murdered.

Victory Conditions

The game continues until the Confederates can no longer advance, or the Union is dispersed and surrenders.

Order of Battle

District of Northeast Louisiana

African Brigade Col. Hermann Lieb [+0]	ES	20	30	40	50	100	Status	Arm.
	1,148	57	38	29	23	11		
9th Louisiana AD (African Descent)	285	14	10	7	6	3	1	M
11th Louisiana AD	482	24	16	12	10	5	1	M
13th Louisiana, 1st Mississippi AD	261	13	9	7	5	3	1	M
23rd Iowa*	120	6	4	3	2	1	3	R

*May attach themselves to another regiment

Col. Isaac F. Shepard [+1]*

*Garrison commander, but under arrest. May not give orders or be used for command and control, but may use his officer benefit to encourage and help units.

Ships

	ES	Status	Armament
U.S.S. Choctaw		3	**1x** 9" SB, **1x** 30 lb. Rifle per side.*
U.S.S. Lexington		3	**2x** 8" Dahlgren SB, **1x** 32 lb. SB per side.*

*Treat as an 8" Columbiad and 30 lb. P.

	ES	Status
Mules	4	-

District of West Louisiana

Walker's Division

McCulloch's Brigade BG Henry E. McCulloch [+1]	ES	20	30	40	50	100	Status	Arm.
	1,504	75	50	38	30	15		
16th Texas	415	21	14	10	8	4	2	M
17th Texas	374	19	12	9	7	4	2	M
19th Texas	393	20	13	10	8	4	2	M
16th Texas Cavalry (Dismounted)	322	16	11	8	6	3	2	M

Brigadier General Henry E. McCulloch

Optional Rules

There are no optional rules for this game, other than the alternate configuration of the above mentioned hasty works on the north flank.

Author's Notes

This is a quirky little game with all sorts of interesting special rules. Gunboats, mule herds, African American soldiers. It's a quick, easy, and unique game.

The modern battlefield is now on private land, and inaccessible. There are no pictures of the battlefield itself available.

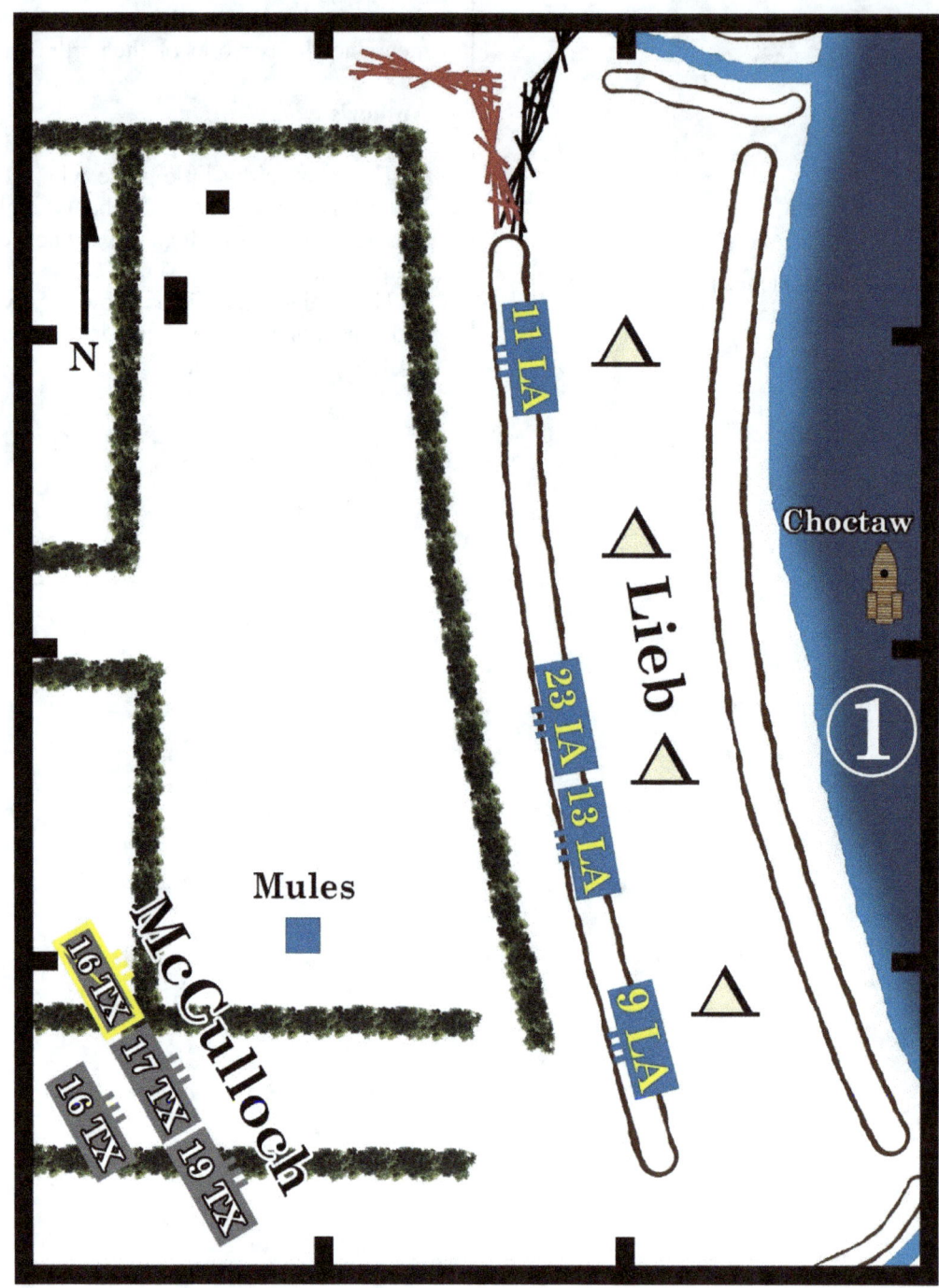

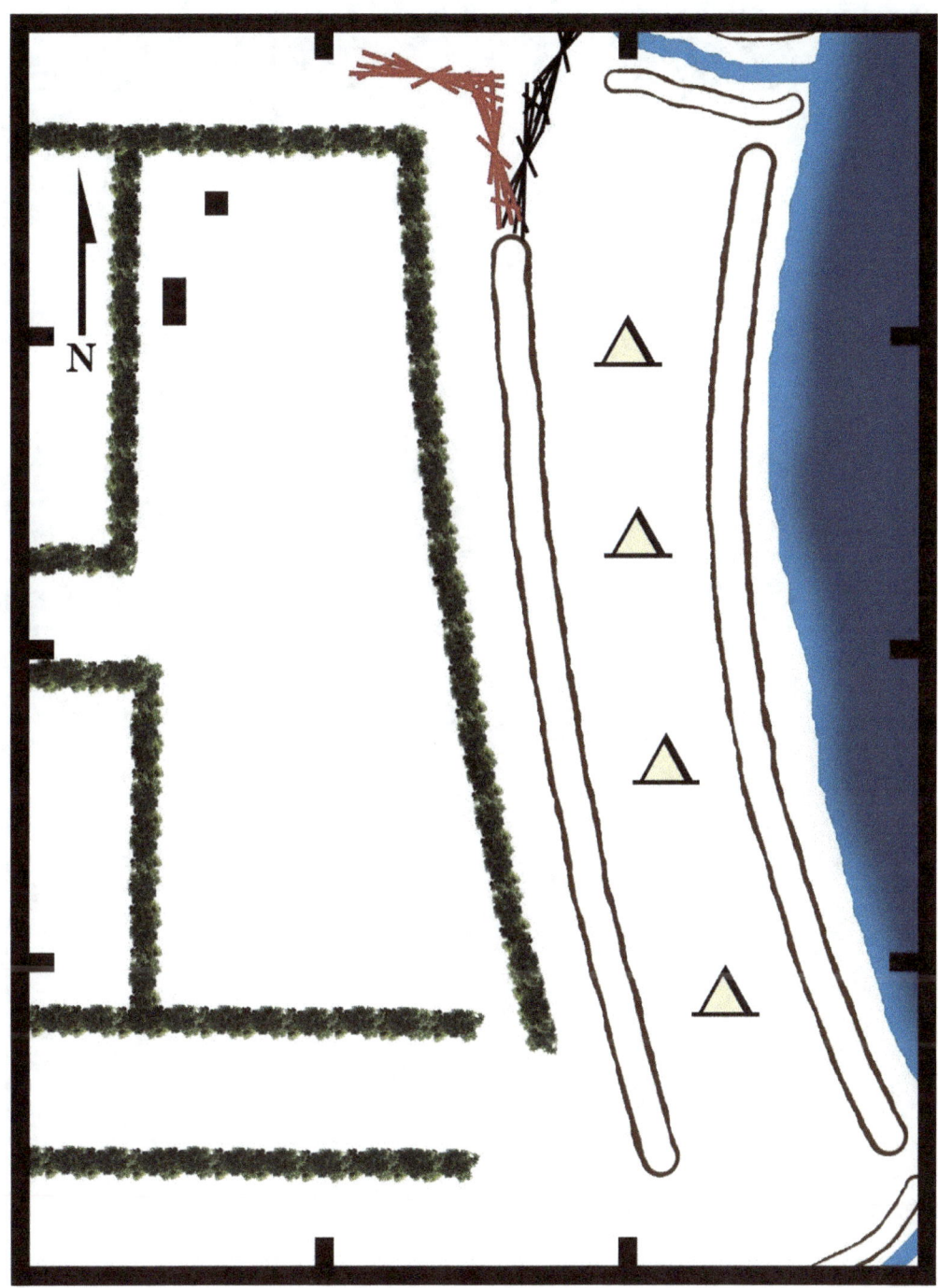

The Battle of Lake Providence
June 9th, 1863

Background

As the attack against Milliken's Bend was unfolding, the other prongs against Union forces west of the Mississippi river continued. General Taylor sent the 13th Texas Cavalry (Dismounted) to the Lake Providence area, about 27 miles upriver, to reinforce Brigadier General Paul O. Hébert and the Confederates in that area. They were to attack the outpost at Lake Providence, which was serving as a small supply base, as well as training newly deserted slaves into Union soldiers, much like Milliken's Bend.

General Hébert had a wide ranging area to command, and was only able to allocate the 13th Louisiana Cavalry Battalion and a single 6 lb. gun to the expedition, along with the newly arrived 13th Texas Cavalry. This combined force under Colonel Frank Bartlett gathered at Floyd, Louisiana where a bridge was being rebuilt over Bayou Macon. However, Bartlett believed this direct route to Lake Providence was in poor condition, and the terrain easily defensible by a small force. He elected to move north to Caledonia, where another bridge was being constructed. This delay cost them two days.

When Bartlett's force approached Bayou Baxter they encountered two companies of the 1st Kansas Mounted Infantry. Although they forced the Kansans back, messengers were able to warn the garrison commander at Lake Providence, Brigadier General Hugh T. Reid. Reid immediately marched west to intercept Bartlett. The Kansans continued to fall back under pressure from the mounted 13th Louisiana Cavalry Battalion, burning the bridge at Bayou Tensas. There Bartlett briefly halted to let the 13th Texas Cavalry, dismounted and on foot, catch up. In addition to pushing the Kansans back, Bartlett captured several supply wagons and mules. However, this delay allowed Reid to arrive.

Bartlett was in the middle of rebuilding the burned bridge when the 16th Wisconsin and 1st Kansas fired into them, as well as the cannon guarding the bridge. The infantry fire forced the

Brigadier General Hugh T. Reid

cannoneers to abandon the gun after firing five shots. Both sides kept up a lively fire across the Bayou for the remainder of the day. At dusk Reid withdrew. His rear guard at the bridge was overwhelmed and driven back by the 8th Louisiana (African Descent), and the battle ended.

Bartlett's delay allowed Reid to arrive on the scene and attack, although without the bridge his only artillery would not have been able to cross Bayou Tensas. The Confederate commander only withdrew because he believed he was outnumbered, when in truth, the two sides were about evenly matched. Ultimately, this movement against an isolated Union outpost on the west bank failed, as did the others at Milliken's Bend and Young's Point. Grant reinforced the men here, and on June 15th advanced on Walker at Richmond. After a brief skirmish, the Texans withdrew from the theater. The threat against the west bank of the Mississippi ended. The only hope for relief of Vicksburg now lay to the east.

Game Overview

This is a small game with a variety of units. Infantry, cavalry, mounted infantry, and artillery. It would make a great introductory scenario, or to test new rules.

The map is small, only 2' x 3'. The game begins at 2 p.m. and ends when one side must withdraw.

Looking east from behind Bartlett's position towards Bayou Tensas. The bayou and bridge are along the tree line.

Terrain

The terrain for this game is flat, with no elevations. Bayou Tensas cuts across the map. It is rough terrain for crossing. The swamps are rough terrain as well. The woods are light woods for movement and visibility. The bridge is destroyed and has no effect on the game.

Deployment

Set up as shown on the scenario map. All units begin the game dismounted. The 1st Kansas Mounted Infantry and the 13th Louisiana Cavalry Battalion may mount and dismount normally. The 13th Texas Cavalry (Dismounted) does not have horses and acts as infantry for the entire game. The Confederates only have one cannon, but if the minimum artillery unit in the game rules is one section, then use that instead.

The 8th Louisiana (African Descent) enters along the road at **1** on Turn [8/6/5]. If the 8th engages in melee or hand-to-hand combat with the enemy, add a small casualty bonus. Depending on the rules, it could be a +1 to a die roll, or a shift up one column. This applies to both sides, and reflects the hatred of both participants.

Victory Conditions

The game continued until one side has to withdraw. If there is no clear winner, add together the Victory Points for enemy units eliminated. The side with the most Victory Points wins.

Reid's approach to the bridge over Bayou Tensas

Order of Battle

Army of the Tennessee

Seventeenth Army Corps
6th Division

2nd Brigade	ES	20	30	40	50	100	Status	Arm.
BG Hugh T. Reid [+1]	913	46	30	23	18	9		
1st Kansas Mounted Infantry	335	17	11	8	7	3	3	R
16th Wisconsin	278	14	9	7	6	3	3	R
8th Louisiana (African Descent)	300	15	10	8	6	3	1	M

District of West Louisiana

Walker's Division

Haws' Brigade	ES	20	30	40	50	100	Status	Arm.
Col. Frank Bartlett [+1]	791	40	26	20	16	8		
13th Texas Cavalry (Dismounted)	486	24	16	12	10	5	3	R
13th Louisiana Cavalry Bn.*	305	15	10	8	6	3	3	C

*Temporarily attached.

Artillery	ES	Status	Armament
Battery		3	**1x** 6 lb. SB

Optional Rules

There are no optional rules for this game.

Author's Notes

This is a small battle that was fought in the middle of nowhere, Louisiana. It gives a good mix of units, and will make a good introductory game for new players, or to test a new set of rules. I like including these small, lesser known battles in scenario books. Not every fight in the civil war was a division or corps affair.

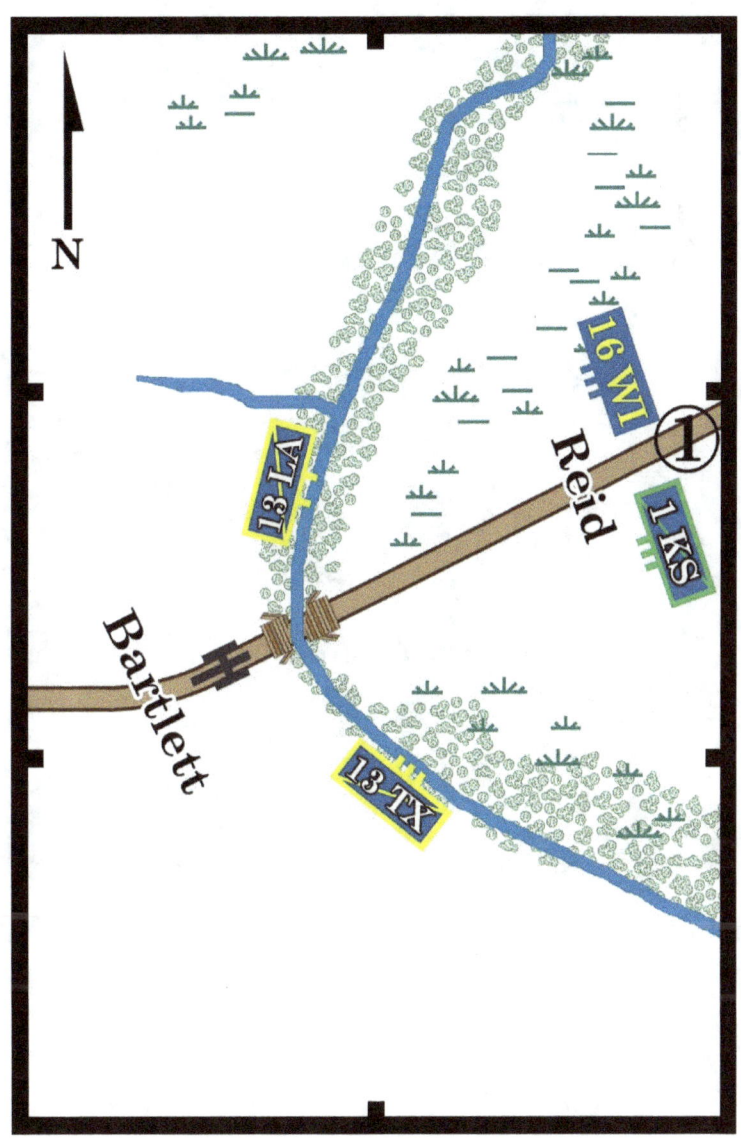

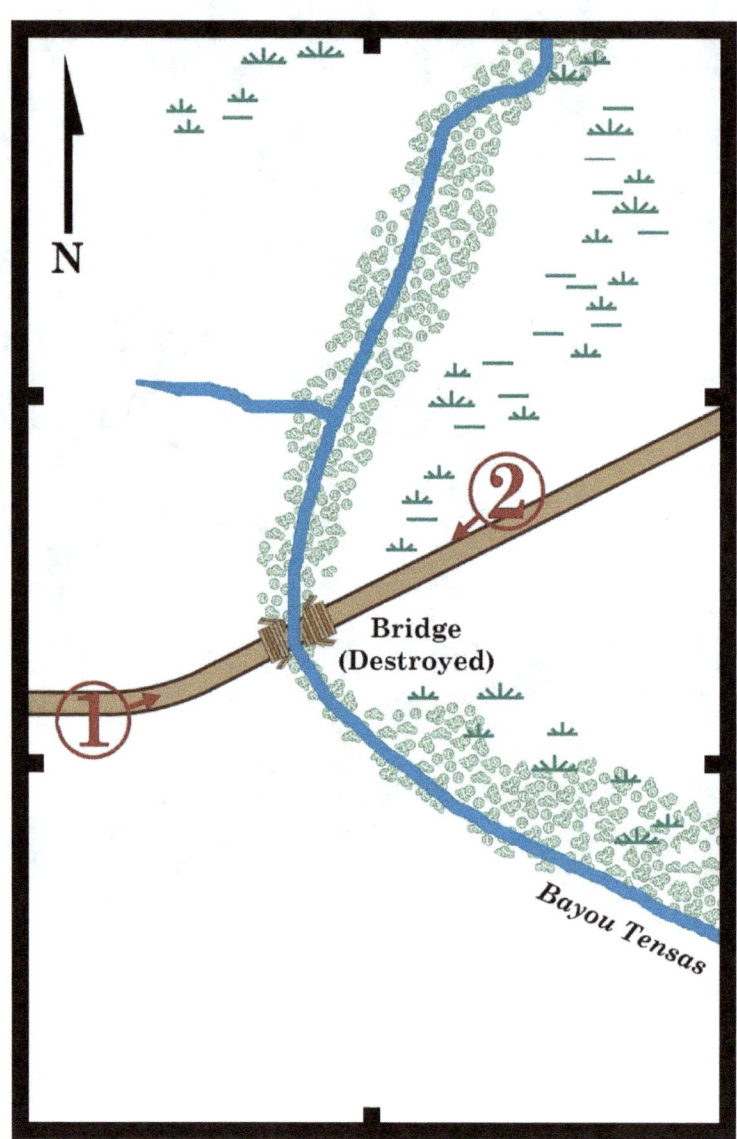

The Battle of Helena
July 4th, 1863

Background

The Union occupation of Helena, Arkansas had threatened the Confederate hold on that state since it's captured by the Federals in July 1862. Located on the Mississippi River 53 miles south of Memphis, and 160 miles north of Vicksburg, the presence of Union soldiers there threatened the interior of Arkansas and made the capital at Little Rock vulnerable to capture. It also served as a supply base for river traffic, provided troops for the Vicksburg siege, and secured northeast Arkansas for the Union.

General Joseph E. Johnston suggested using forces west of the Mississippi to relive the siege of Vicksburg. Previous attempts at Richmond, Louisiana had failed. Trans-Mississippi Department commander Lieutenant General Edmund Kirby Smith deferred the idea of an attack on Helena to Lieutenant General Theophilus H. Holmes, who commanded the District of Arkansas. Holmes thought the garrison too strong to attack. However, when word reached him in mid-June that the garrison had been weakened to provide reinforcements for Grant, he decided to concentrate his forces and capture the town. He would link up with men under Major General Sterling Price, and move to Helena. Holmes, who still had reservations against the move, relented when Price agreed to publicly support his decision if the attack failed. Unfortunately for Holmes, the terrain and weather conspired against a quick attack. It was not until July 3rd when the disparate forces in the department rendezvoused outside of Helena.

The defenses at Helena were formidable. The town was surrounded by imposing hills with sheer, steep slopes. The garrison was commanded by Major General Benjamin M. Prentiss, of Shiloh fame. The center of the defense was Fort Curtis. However, when word arrived of the approaching Confederates Prentiss ordered new forts built on the high ground west of town. Four new batteries were constructed, trees cleared to provide fields of fire, and the debris used to create an abatis to

Major General Benjamin M. Prentiss

delay the attackers. With the rebels drawing near, Prentiss cancelled the Fourth of July celebration, and ordered the roads from the west blocked with trees and barricades. The *U.S.S. Tyler* stood offshore to provide additional fire support.

Holmes' battle plan was complicated. It required the army's cavalry to attack from the north, Price's Division to attack from the east, and Brigadier General James F. Fagan's Brigade, under Holmes' direct supervision, to attack from the southwest. The terrain and clogged roads slowed everyone down. The battle began to the south before daylight, along the Lower Little Rock Road, when a Confederate force encountered Union pickets. Fagan attacked next at dawn, struggling to assault Battery D and its supporting infantry. Price misunderstood Holmes' orders, and did not attack at the same time. This allowed the Union to concentrate their artillery and reinforcements to repulse Fagan. To the north, the Confederate cavalry's advance was lukewarm at best, and never really developed into a full scale attack.

Holmes moved to correct Price, and his attack got underway at 7 a.m. The blocked roads prevented any of the army's artillery from moving to the front, so it was an infantry affair. Price's men overran the pickets, and after a sharp fight, captured Battery C. However, once on that high ground they were stuck. Converging fire from Batteries B and D, Fort Curtis, and the *Tyler* pinned down Price. Attempts to move down the

View of the interior of Battery C.

hill towards the town were met with overwhelming firepower. With the rebel cavalry doing nothing but skirmishing, Prentiss was able to shift some reinforcements from the north to assist.

Holmes couldn't get the attacks coordinated. He would often give orders contradictory to Price. A mistaken attack directly towards Fort Curtis was shredded by Union artillery. Attempts to coordinate attacks on Battery D failed. At 10:30 a.m. Holmes realized further attempts were fruitless. He ordered his army to withdraw. Helena was safe, and the last attempt to influence the siege of Vicksburg failed. In fact, unknown to the battle's participants, Vicksburg surrendered that very day. As President Lincoln remarked, "the Father of the Waters again goes unvexed to the sea."

Game Overview

This game is a twist for this book, with the Confederates having to attack the Union behind fortifications. The rebels will have to negotiate unfavorable terrain, and attack and drive the Union from the heights, and hopefully recapture Helena for the Confederacy.

The game board is 4' x 6' in size. The game begins at dawn at 4:00 a.m. and ends when the Confederacy can no longer attack, or the Union is driven from the board.

Terrain

The game board is a little complex, with a series of very sharp terrain to the west, and the flat and level town of Helena to the east. The hills to the west are very steep. In person they are almost cliffs. Each level should be 1" tall, and should be very steep. All slopes are rough terrain. The woods are broken terrain. Visibility is for light woods.

The creeks only deduct an inch from movement. The canal is rough terrain for infantry and cavalry, but is impassable to artillery expect at the bridges. The swamp is rough terrain. Fences deduct an inch from movement. The town and streets of Helena are laid out in a basic fashion. Players may want to add more fences for visual flavor. The cornfield only provides a cover (or concealment) bonus for units lying prone. The corn isn't yet tall enough to completely hide a unit moving through it.

The Union forts are heavy works. The connecting trenches are medium works. There is

Lieutenant General Theophilus H. Holmes

an abatis covering most of the frontage. The roads are clogged with debris and additional abatis. They are rough terrain for infantry, and impassable for artillery. A Confederate infantry unit may spend one turn removing the blockage. At the end of the turn an amount equal to the frontage of the regiment may be removed.

Deployment

Begin the game set up as shown. Batteries B, C, and D have clear views towards each other and can see the cleared space in front of their sister batteries. The range may be a little long, but they should be able to fire at any enemy unit approaching the neighboring fort. Likewise, Fort Curtis has a clear view up the slope and to the back of each battery. Fire on level ground is blocked by any houses, as normal, but Fort Curtis can see above the houses to any higher elevation to the west. The guns in Fort Curtis have a 360 degree firing arc. The ramparts and barbette carriages were specifically made chest high to allow for this. General Prentiss begins the game in Fort Curtis. General Salomon can begin anywhere on the board next to a Federal unit.

The 1st Indiana Cavalry arrives at **1** in march column on Turn [14/10/8]. The *U.S.S. Tyler* is off the board to the east and can provide artillery fire. Place a marker on the eastern edge of the board indicating the gunboats relative position. Use that marker to calculate line of sight and determine any firing from that point. Add an extra foot to the firing distance to replicate the extra additional space to the river. The *Tyler* may "move" one foot in either direction per turn. It does not suffer any penalties for firing while moving. The *Tyler* has a clear line of sight to any unit on a higher elevation. However, on the lowest street level its line of sight is blocked by any buildings. Essentially confining it to shooting down the streets, and only if it happens to be aligned along a street at that moment.

If the 2nd Arkansas Colored Infantry engages in melee or hand-to-hand combat with the enemy, add a small casualty bonus. Depending on the rules, it could be a +1 to a die roll, or a shift up one column. This applies to both sides, and reflects the hatred of both participants.

For the Confederates, the 34th Arkansas and Blocker's Arkansas Battery enter at **2** on Turn [7/5/4]. They can be in any formation, whether in march column along the road or in line of battle. Price's Division enters on Turn [10/7/5]. McRae's Brigade enters at **3** in line of battle. Parson's enters at **4** in line of battle. The 9th Battalion Missouri Sharpshooters should be in front in a skirmish line. General Price and the artillery for both brigades enters along the road between them. They can either move off-road from there, into the difficult terrain, or they can wait for an infantry unit to be allocated to clear the road. Either way, it's going to be difficult to get the artillery engaged, but that's how it was historically.

As the fighting wore on, General Holmes and Price began issuing contradictory orders to their men. To reflect this, after Turn [14/10/8] any order issued to a unit within a 6 inch diameter of Holmes (3 inches in any direction) has a 50% chance of being cancelled. The exception is if Holmes is touching the unit, in which case it will be assumed that Holmes himself issued the order. To further make things interesting, instead of cancelling the order, players could make a chart beforehand and roll for a random order result issued instead. Because of this limitation, players might be tempted to shuffle Holmes away to some far corner of the board. This is a legitimate option, but Holmes can still rally disordered or routed units despite his low bonus, so it may be worth it to keep him around.

Victory Conditions

The battle continued until the Confederates can no longer advance using the rules for command and control, or the Union is forced from the board and surrenders.

Order of Battle

District of Eastern Arkansas
MG Benjamin M. Prentiss [+2]

Cavalry Brigade	ES	20	30	40	50	100	Status	Arm.
1st Indiana Cavalry	397	20	13	10	8	4	3	BC

Unattached	ES	20	30	40	50	100	Status	Arm.
2nd Arkansas Colored Infantry	342	17	11	9	7	3	1	R

Artillery Battalion	ES	Status	Armament
3rd Iowa Battery	94	3	**1x** 6 lb. SB, **1x** 12 lb. H
Battery K, 1st Missouri	92	3	**4x** 10 lb. P

Forts	ES	Status	Armament
Battery B		3	**1x** 6 lb. SB, **1x** 12 lb. H
Battery C		3	**1x** 6 lb. SB, **1x** 12 lb. H
Battery D		3	**1x** 6 lb. JR, **1x** 6 lb. SB, **1x** 12 lb. H
Fort Curtis		3	**6x** 32 lb. SB, **1x** 42 lb. SB

Thirteenth Army Corps (attached and reports to District of Eastern Arkansas)
Thirteenth Division
BG Frederick Salomon [+2]*
*Given tactical control by Prentiss. May confer his benefit to any Union unit on the board.

1st Brigade	ES	20	30	40	50	100	Status	Arm.
Col. William E. McLean [+1]	1,319	66	44	33	26	13		
43rd Indiana	421	21	14	11	8	4	3	R
35th, 33rd Missouri	414	21	14	10	8	4	3	R
28th Wisconsin	484	24	16	12	10	5	3	R

2nd Brigade	ES	20	30	40	50	100	Status	Arm.
Col. Samuel A. Rice [+1]	470	24	16	12	9	5		
33rd Iowa	470	24	16	12	9	5	2	R

	ES	Status	Armament
USS Tyler		3	**3x** 8" SB, **1x** 30 lb. P per side.

Looking across the interior of Fort Curtis looking southwest. The hills surrounding the town are visible in the background. It's easy to see why the artillery in the fort had an all-around field of fire.

District of Arkansas

LG Theophilus H. Holmes [+1]

Fagan's Brigade*	ES	20	30	40	50	100	Status	Arm.
BG James F. Fagan [+1]	1,339	67	45	33	27	13		
34th Arkansas	277	14	9	7	6	3	3	R
35th Arkansas	302	15	10	8	6	3	3	R
37th Arkansas	432	22	14	11	9	4	3	R
Hawthorne's Arkansas Infantry	328	16	11	8	7	3	3	R
	ES	Status	Armament					
Blocker's Arkansas Battery		3	2x 6 lb. SB					

*No division commander. Reports directly to Holmes.

Scene of the south end of the battlefield. The two story house is the home of General Thomas C. Hindman. Battery D is visible on the hill in the left background.

Price's Division
MG Sterling Price [+2]

McRae's Brigade	ES	20	30	40	50	100	Status	Arm.
BG Dandridge McRae [+1]	1,143	57	38	29	23	11		
32nd Arkansas	357	18	12	9	7	4	2	R
36th Arkansas	381	19	13	10	8	4	3	R
39th Arkansas	405	20	14	10	8	4	3	R

	ES	Status	Armament
Marshall's Arkansas Battery		3	**2x** 6 lb. SB, **2x** 12 lb. H

Parson's Brigade	ES	20	30	40	50	100	Status	Arm.
BG Mosby M. Parsons [+1]	1,784	89	59	45	36	18		
7th Missouri	451	23	15	11	9	5	3	R
8th Missouri	497	25	17	12	10	5	3	R
9th Missouri	187	9	6	5	4	2	3	M
10th Missouri	447	22	15	11	9	4	3	M
9th Bn. Missouri Sharpshooters	203	10	7	5	4	2	2	R

	ES	Status	Armament
3rd Missouri Battery		3	**2x** 6 lb. SB, **2x** 12 lb. H

Optional Rules

One rule is to disregard the contradictory order rules for Holmes, but this might take a way a bit of the fun.

Author's Notes

This is such an interesting battle. The Confederates are on the attack in this one, and up against earthworks. They have the numbers advantage, but the terrain is horrible. The Union looks weak, and they are. The forts are formidable, but the artillery manning them isn't exactly state of the art. Still, Fort Curtis is very strong, and a solid anchor for the defense even if one or two of the outer batteries is overrun. Regardless, it's going to take skill for the Union to prevail. If you like a challenge, play the Union in this game.

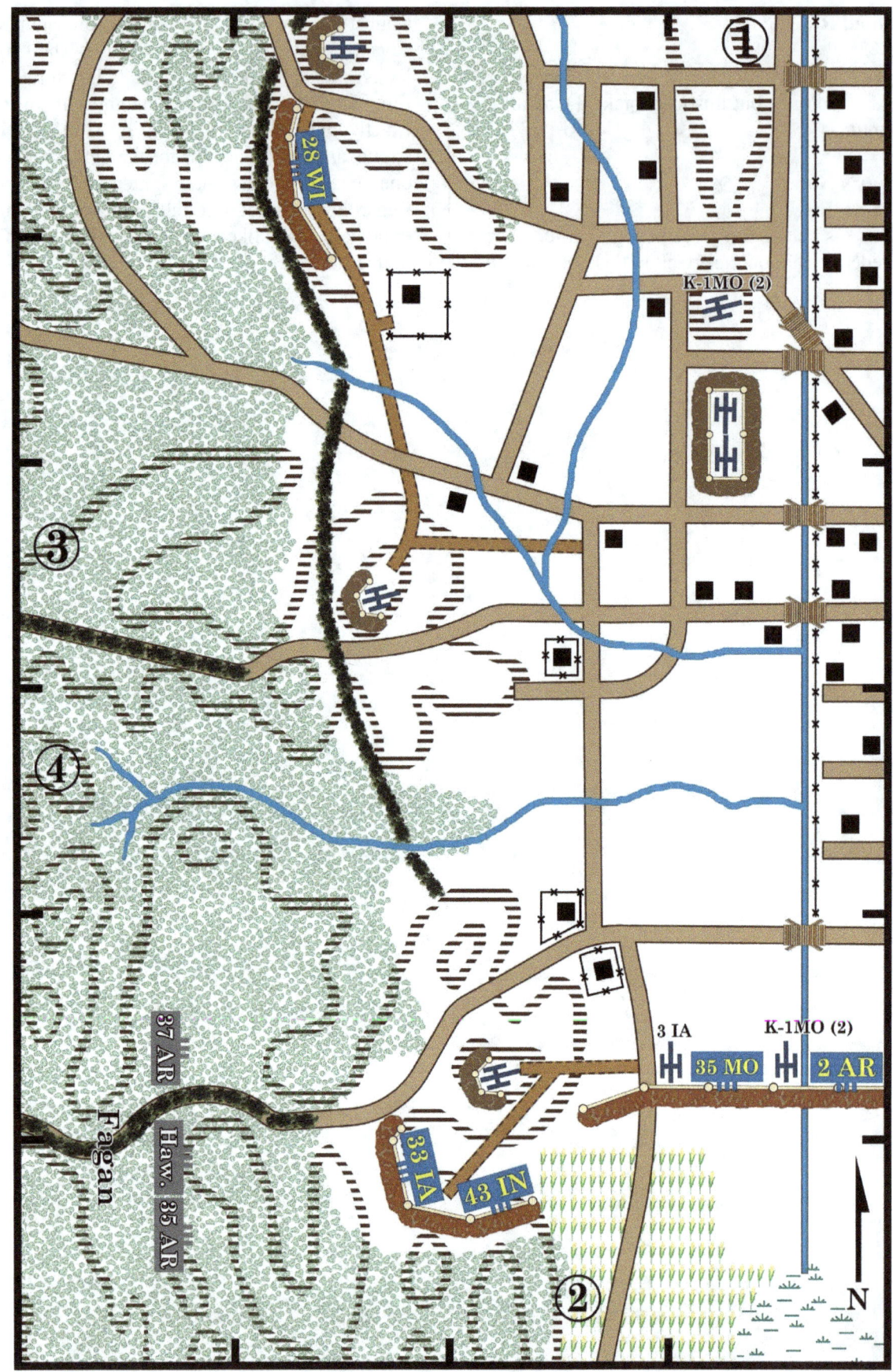

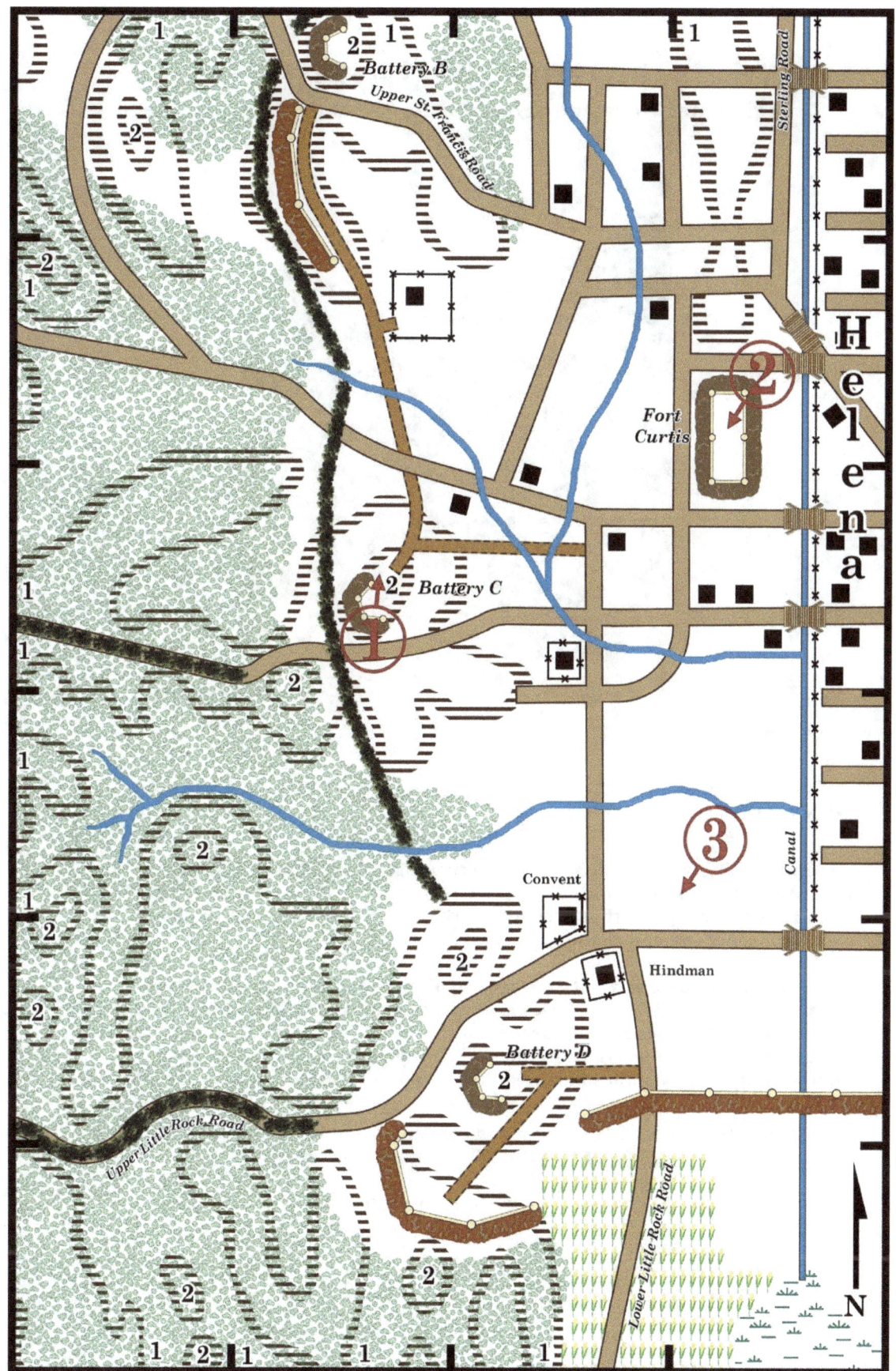

Summer Storm:
Regimental Wargame Scenarios for the Battle of Gettysburg

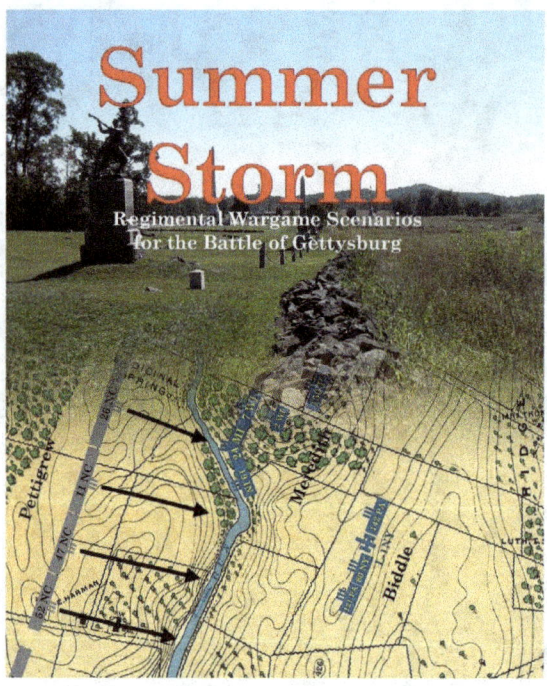

Stock # HI0006

ISBN 13: 978-0-9904122-4-3

The Battle of Gettysburg was one of the turning points of the American Civil War. The Peach Orchard, Devil's Den, and Little Round Top were made famous by the struggles that occured there. Refight the battle on the game table and see if you can change the course of history!

These scenarios are designed for use with almost any American Civil War regimental level set of rules. Rules are included for figures based on 20, 30, 40, 50, and 100 historic men per figure/stand. Times are given for 10, 15, and 20 minutes per game turn. Maps are in full color, as are the numerous color photographs of the modern battlefield. Does not include miniature wargame rules.

Available late January 2016 at Amazon.com, other online retailers, as well as your local gaming store (with the ISBN number above).

Also available for download at www.wargamevault.com

This Bloody Field:
Regimental Wargame Scenarios for the Battle of Shiloh

Stock # HI0009

ISBN 10: 0-9904122-7-4

ISBN 13: 978-0-9904122-7-4

The Battle of Shiloh was the first truly large battle in the American Civil War's western theatre, and the largest until Chickamauga the next year. With largely inexperienced troops, the two sides faced each other and knocked each other around until one withdrew from sheer exhaustion. Try your hand at the gaming table and manage the chaos of untried and untested combat troops thrown together and pitted against each other in a fight to the death along the Tennessee River!

These scenarios are designed for use with almost any American Civil War regimental level set of rules. Rules are included for figures based on 20, 30, 40, 50, and 100 historic men per figure/stand. Times are given for 10, 15, and 20 minutes per game turn. Maps are in full color, as are the numerous color photographs of the modern battlefield. Does not include miniature wargame rules.

Available at Amazon.com, other online retailers, as well as your local gaming store (with the ISBN numbers above).

Also available for download at www.wargamevault.com

Unflinching Courage:
Regimental Wargame Scenarios for the Coastal Campaigns: 1862-1865

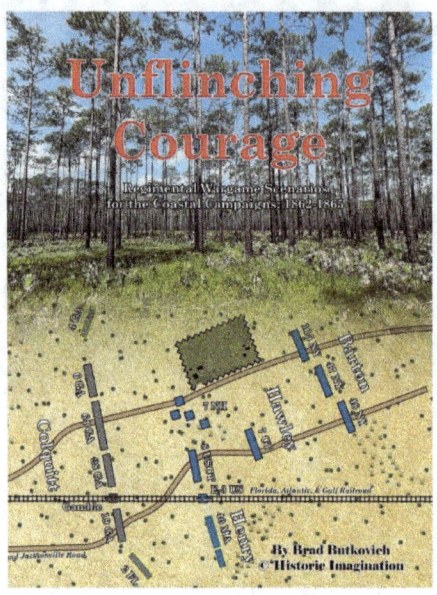

Stock # HI0019

ISBN 13: 979-8-9904149-0-7

While much of the fighting during the American Civil War focused on the struggles in Virginia, Tennessee, Georgia, and along the Mississippi River, the sea line coastal states were not left untouched. Port cities brought vital supplies into the Confederacy from overseas. Critical railroads and infrastructure crossed through and connected the disparate parts of the South, and vital industries supplied the armies of rebellion. The Union was quick to take action against these, blockading port, capturing them when possible, and raiding the interior to destroy railroads and factories. This scenario book contains rules to simulate nine battles fought along the Atlantic coastline from 1862-1865.

These miniature wargame scenarios are designed to be used with almost any American Civil War regimental or brigade level set of rules. Rules are included for figures based on 20, 30, 40, 50, and 100 historic men per figure/stand. Times are given for 10, 15, and 20 minutes per game turn. Maps are in full color, as are the numerous color photographs of the modern battlefields.
This book does not contain rules for playing miniature wargames.

Available at Amazon.com, other online retailers, as well as your local gaming store (with the ISBN number above).

Also available for download at www.wargamevault.com

Brave Hearts Trembled:
Regimental Wargame Scenarios for the Battle of Antietam

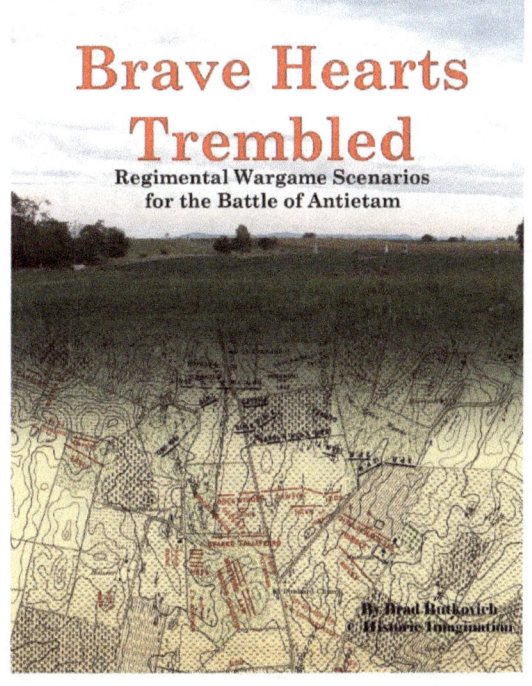

Stock # HI0007

ISBN 10: 0-9904122-5-0

ISBN 13: 978-0-9904122-5-0

The Battle of Antietam was the single bloodiest day in American military history. It was fought with a ferocity unsurpassed by anything the men who battled there encountered before or afterwards! Recreate the struggle to contain the Confederacy's first invasion of the north.

These scenarios are designed for use with almost any American Civil War regimental level set of rules. Rules are included for figures based on 20, 30, 40, 50, and 100 historic men per figure/stand. Times are given for 10, 15, and 20 minutes per game turn. Maps are in full color, as are the numerous color photographs of the modern battlefield. Does not include miniature wargame rules.

Available at Amazon.com, other online retailers, as well as your local gaming store (with the ISBN numbers above).

Also available for download at www.wargamevault.com

Aim Low Boys!:
Regimental Wargame Scenarios in the Shenandoah Valley: 1862-1864

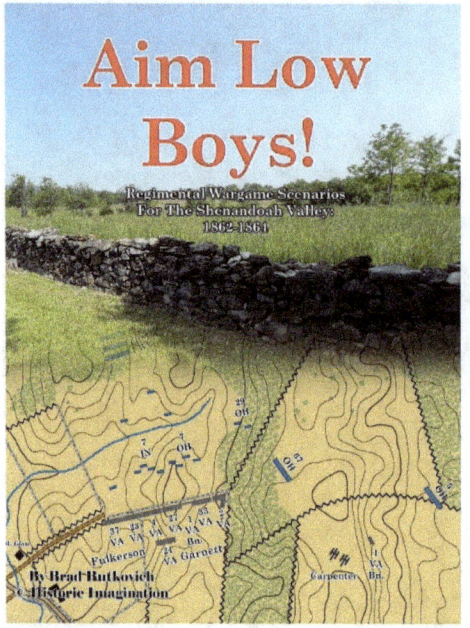

Stock # HI0016

ISBN 13: 978-1-7325976-7-9

The Shenandoah Valley played a pivotal role in the American Civil War in Virginia, always influencing, and being influenced by, the major campaigns being fought in the East. Being a source of food, war materials, and a transportation nexus often brought the once idyllic valley to the forefront of the conflict. Can you stop the Union from destroying this resource? Can you prevent the Confederates from marching towards Washington, D. C. by the back door?

These miniature wargame scenarios are designed to be used with almost any American Civil War regimental or brigade level set of rules. Rules are included for figures based on 20, 30, 40, 50, and 100 historic men per figure/stand. Times are given for 10, 15, and 20 minutes per game turn. Maps are in full color, as are the numerous color photographs of the modern battlefield.
This book does not contain core rules for playing miniature wargames.

Available at Amazon.com, other online retailers, as well as your local gaming store (with the ISBN number above).

Also available for download at www.wargamevault.com

www.ingramcontent.com/pod-product-compliance
Lightning Source LLC
LaVergne TN
LVHW061936070526
838199LV00060B/3845